Because I Love You Sew

ston

17 Handmade Gifts for Everyone in Your Life

stashBOOKS®

an imprint of C&T Publishing

Publisher: Amy Marson

Creative Director: Gailen Runge

Art Director: Kristy Zacharias

Editor: Lynn Koolish

Technical Editors: Debbie Rodgers and Daniel Rouse

Cover/Book Designer: April Mostek

Page Layout Artist: Katie McIntosh

Production Coordinator: Zinnia Heinzmann

Production Editor: Alice Mace Nakanishi

Illustrator: Tim Manibusan

Photo Assistant: Mary Peyton Peppo

Style photography by Britt Lakin, unless otherwise noted; Instructional photography by Diane Pedersen and Nissa Brehmer of C&T Publishing, Inc., unless otherwise noted

Published by Stash Books, an imprint of C&T Publishing, Inc., P.O. Box 1456, Lafayette, CA 94549

Library of Congress Cataloging-in-Publication Data

Preston, Trish, 1971-

  Because I love you sew : 17 handmade gifts for everyone in your life / Trish Preston.

    pages cm

  ISBN 978-1-60705-812-0 (soft cover)

1. Sewing. 2. House furnishings. 3. Dress accessories. 4. Gifts. I. Title.

TT705.P75 2014

646--dc23

                          2013040406

Printed in China

10 9 8 7 6 5 4 3 2 1

Dedication

This book is dedicated to my grandmother, Florence Hendrix Pace, and my sister, Lisa Lynne Raridan. Your talents and love have inspired me my entire life. I feel your hands, even from heaven, in my life and in my work. I love you very much.

Acknowledgments

Thank you to my wonderful friends who helped to create samples, edit, and make my words understandable: Nova Carmen, Joyce Barrett, Jamie Donaghey, and LaNeka Richards.

A million thank-yous to Carla Webb for your love and support. There most likely would not be a Two Peas in a Pod without the tireless help, late-night pep talks, and willingness to come over at a moment's notice from one of my best friends, Kristin Delp. Thank you for everything you do for my family and me.

My Two Peas brand looks so amazing in print thanks to Britt Lakin of Britt Lakin Photography. Words would never suffice to thank you for your friendship and support and your amazing talent.

Thank you to my brother Danny; my sister, Lori; my mother-in-law, Sondra; and my wonderful parents, Bill and Carol. You inspire me, you encourage me, you lift me up when I'm down, you take my kids when I need a break, and you love me even when I screw up. Thank you.

Thank you to my three gifts from God: my daughters, Lauren, Emmalee, and Sophia. You are my reason for everything I do. Thank you for your patience while I was in "book mode" and not "mom mode" and for letting me back in after this job was done to be your mom. There is no job on this earth that means more to me or that I would rather do than be your mom. You each make me so proud. I love you to the moon and back.

And finally, to my husband, Ken—without your help, this book simply would not be. Thank you for taking over and going into full-time Mr. Mom duty during this project. For cooking, cleaning, schlepping kids to a million activities, bringing me snacks to the sewing room, making me coffee, and whispering to me that you are so proud of me when I felt like I couldn't go on. I couldn't do any of what I do without your support. I thank God for bringing you into my life, for making me your wife, and for the life we have together. No storm could ever tear us apart. I love you forever and always.

CONTENTS

Introduction

When I was growing up, my mother crafted a tiny corner in our living room with a side table and a cabinet filled with paper and crayons and paints and yarns and crafty things. As soon as I could hold a crayon in my hand, I would sit there for hours, drawing, painting, coloring, and creating. Finding time as often as I could to craft and create art is something that I have loved all my life.

I can remember the distinct moment when my love of sewing began. It was my fifth birthday—my grandmother made me a doll that was as tall as I was and made me a dress to match the doll's dress. I couldn't believe she made it, and to this day, that doll is one of my all-time favorite gifts ever! In fact, that doll sits in my sewing room watching over me—Grammy's heart is sewn into every stitch, and I love having her close.

For me sewing is spiritual, peaceful, and a connection to people in my life whom I have loved and who are gone. It is also a connection to people I love in my life right now, who inspire me, encourage me, and surround me with an energy that absolutely feeds my soul.

It is the love that both my grandmothers shared with me.

It is the inspiration of eclectic color that my mother introduced me to.

It is the "can do" spirit that my kite-making father showed me.

It is the "I want to be like them" desire that a little sister gets while watching her older sisters sew.

It is the "you are amazing" love a wife has for her husband while she watches him sew Barbie clothes for his baby girls because they asked him to.

It is the passion I'm sharing with my own children. And I hope they not only treasure the moments we spend together, learning to sew, but also remember the stories that go along with each handmade item I've given them.

That spiritual place and profound love for my family is where this book was born—because I love them all *so* much, and I love to show them how much I love them through sewing, using my hands to make them something from my heart.

For each of you reading this book, I hope that these projects inspire you to treasure those special moments in your life and to show others how much you love them so.

About Gift Giving

The idea for this book started right here, from these journal pages about making something special for my girls.

I was a new mom to identical twin girls, and although I hadn't really sewn many garments before (okay, maybe one), I decided I wanted to sew the dresses for their holy baptism. I wanted to make them myself because I so strongly desired to start creating special keepsakes for both my girls, something that they would give to their kids. And that's been my heart's desire when it comes to sewing most everything—to make something special for someone that I love so very much.

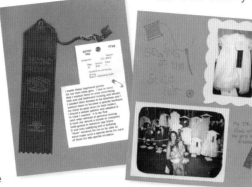

I really like the idea of provenance, the recording and keeping of the history of something. It was important for me not only to make these dresses but also to record the process and the event for which they wore them. I have photos of me making them with help from their godmother, Irene. I have all the family photos of the girls wearing these dresses at church, with our pastor and all our family.

Later, my mom encouraged me to enter their dresses into the Ohio State Fair sewing competition, and I did. That's the photo you see above when the girls were two years old and we went to see the dresses on display at the fair. I won second place—so what if there were only two entries in the category. I got a cool ribbon and a great story from it. My mom visited the fair before us and she didn't know there were only two entries in my category—she just saw I got second place. She was so excited and proud! So was I, quite frankly.

Both my twins sew on their own now. They are in 4-H and compete in sewing competitions at our local county fair. We keep a scrapbook of the entire process and what they've made. I'll keep all of it to share with their kids one day.

I encourage you to do the same. Keep scraps of fabric from your projects. Write about why you made the item and who you made it for. Include pictures of the special day. Maybe even clip those stories inside the cover of this book so that someday you can give this book to someone you love, with stories about what you created, and encourage them to sew for someone they love so very much.

One of the beautiful things that an artist does when they complete their work is to sign it. Using a computer-printable fabric sheet, you can create your very own signature handmade labels to sew into your projects. I've created a file that you can download and customize with your name and the year. These labels make a great addition and special touch to your handmade gift. You can find the label and more ideas and resources for digital journaling your sewing journey on my website (see Resources, page 111).

The Two Peas today, holding their baptismal gowns

Family Tree Crazy Quilt

Finished quilt: 34½″ × 34½″
Finished block: 11½″ × 11½″

My sweet mother did not learn to sew until she was, let's just say, much later in life. (I may not be invited for Christmas dinner if I actually share her age.) There was a contest in our hometown, a suburb of Dayton, Ohio, to celebrate the city's anniversary. Quilters were invited to depict the anniversary of the Wright brothers' first flight. My mother, along with my father, created a crazy quilt and incorporated photos throughout of the Wright brothers. (My dad is really the mastermind behind my mother's projects and a pretty darn good kite designer and sewist.)

My mom took first place. She was so proud and excited, as was all our family. That fabulous quilt was the inspiration for this *Family Tree Crazy Quilt* project.

The best part of this project was working together with my dad to come up with the pattern. He is an engineer by trade, so his mathematical genius came in quite handy. We labored over how to piece each block and made a mess of Mom's kitchen table in the process. His engineer brain and my artsy brain make for a pretty good match.

As with many things, it is the process rather than the end result that is important. In this case, my family and I loved this quilt when we were done making it, but even more I loved making it together with my dad. *That* is the essence of handmade—sharing, loving, and making memories.

This version of a crazy quilt is crazy in its design, but does use a pattern and is paper-foundation pieced to make it easy to put together. The blocks create an abstract image of a tree, and along with your family photos that you print on fabric, you'll have your own *Family Tree Crazy Quilt* wallhanging.

This quilt makes a fabulous wedding or anniversary gift, but you can also theme this quilt in many different ways for many different celebrations.

Construction

Make the Blocks

1. Photocopy or trace the block pattern (pullout page P1) 9 times. I suggest that you make notes on each block indicating the colors to use, referring to the quilt assembly diagram (page 12).

2. Cut each fabric piece about ¾˝ larger than the pattern piece on all sides.

3. Piece the block in numerical order, noting which color fabric should be used for each piece in each block:

- Pin fabric piece 1, right side up, on the blank side of the printed block. Hold the paper up to the light to make sure the fabric is fully covering the piece 1 shape and that there is at least a ¼″ seam allowance all the way around.

- Pin piece 2, wrong side up, on the blank side of the printed block, on top of piece 1 at the seam allowance line.

- Sew on the printed side of the paper along the seamline between pieces 1 and 2.

- Fold back paper at the seam allowance and trim the seam to ¼″.

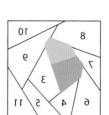

- Open out piece 2 and press.
- Repeat for remaining pieces to complete block.

4. When all the blocks are made, carefully remove the paper, and trim to 12″ square.

Put It Together

Seam allowances are ¼˝.

1. Arrange the blocks, making sure to orient each block correctly to create the tree image as shown in the quilt assembly diagram (page 12).

2. Sew the blocks into 3 rows of 3 blocks each. Press these seams in alternate directions so they nest when the rows are sewn together.

3. Sew together the rows. Press.

4. Prepare and print your photos on the printable fabric sheets, following the manufacturer's instructions. Keep in mind that the photos will be trimmed to about a 3˝ or 4˝ circle, or whatever size you have chosen.

Tip

For best results, use photo-editing software to adjust your photos as needed. Keep in mind that fabric absorbs some of the ink, so it's a good idea to increase the saturation and print a test photo before you print all your photos.

5. Cut each photo into a circle about 3˝ or 4˝ diameter, using a jar lid or other circle as a template.

6. Place the apples around the tree. You may pin them or use the fusible web to hold them in place. Place the printed photos on top of the apples and pin in place. If desired, arrange felt leaves and stitch onto the quilt top. You can also add quilting as you choose.

7. Using a zigzag, satin, or other appliqué stitch, sew the photos and apples to the quilt top.

Finish

1. With right sides facing, sew together the backing fabric along one of the 35″ edges, leaving a 10″ opening in the center. Press seam to one side.

2. Pin and baste optional ties, evenly spaced across, to the top of the backing (see *Oh Baby! Quilted Wallhanging*, Make the Ties, page 18) if desired.

3. Place the quilt right side up on the batting.

4. Place the quilt backing on the quilt top, right sides facing. Pin and sew around all the edges using a walking foot, if available. Trim the corners.

5. Turn the quilt right side out by pulling it through opening in the quilt back. Carefully use the point of your scissors or the blunt end of another tool to poke out the corners crisply. Hand stitch to close the opening. Press.

6. Quilt lines on the tree trunk and limbs, as well as leaves in the green areas, swirls in the sky, or any pattern you wish.

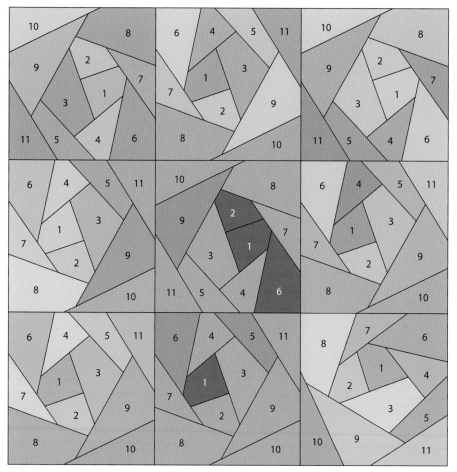

Quilt assembly

Because I Love You Sew

Little Gems

Whenever I meet people at different sewing events, I always share that I'm what I would call "an advanced beginner" sewist. They usually look at me with this "Oh, you're just being humble" kind of look. Even though I've been sewing for more than 20 years, I'm still learning. And I love that I haven't even begun to know everything there is to know about sewing. It keeps me challenged and hungry to learn more. One of my favorite moments to learn is when I sit down and sew with friends.

We live on a rural road, and I'm lucky in that I have several crafty friends and neighbors who live within about a mile of our house. One of them is Joyce. Her daughter is in my twins club, which is how we met. Joyce is also the founder of our town's local quilt guild, and she helped me with the quilt projects in this book. As we spent time working on these projects together, Joyce kept sharing little gems of sewing secrets that I loved adding to my own stash of sewing knowledge. I asked Joyce to share a few of those secrets and ideas with you.

For the *Family Tree Crazy Quilt*:

Joyce Barrett

- Try free-motion thread painting to create the bark on the tree.

- Shorten the stitch length/width to satin stitch around the apples. Or use a blanket stitch and black thread to give it a folk-art look.

- The sew-in computer fabric sheets for the photos can also be used to print birth announcements, wedding invitations, or other family documents for the quilt.

Oh Baby!
Quilted Wallhanging

Finished wallhanging: 17″ × 17″
Finished block: 8″ × 8″

You know that moment when you go to put on your little one's favorite shirt and realize they grew about 6″ overnight and their shirt now resembles something like a bikini top. And then you get that sad feeling that they are growing way, way too fast. And even though they have outgrown that shirt, you can't bear to part with it. You just sit there on the floor and snuggle that shirt for a moment, and then snuggle your little one. I'm kind of sentimental like that, so please tell me you've shared that moment too?

Savoring those moments and finding a sweet way to hold on to them is what inspired this project. Using your little one's outgrown clothes, you can create a wallhanging that will capture those moments forever. We've used rainbow colors in this project to make it gender neutral, but you can change the colors to anything your heart desires.

This could be altered for an adult as well and makes an amazing heartfelt gift as a memory quilt wallhanging. I have one in the works on my sewing table. A stack of my grandfather's golf shirts sits in my unfinished projects pile (the man lived and breathed to golf every day of his wonderful life), and I'm using the embroidered logos from his shirts to piece into a wallhanging.

MATERIALS

T-SHIRTS: 4, each with fun designs or logos (Image should be smaller than 5″ × 5″.)

BRIGHT COLORS: scraps or ⅛ yard each for sashing (I used orange, yellow, green, teal, purple, and red.)

GRAY: ½ yard (includes border and backing)

LIGHTWEIGHT FUSIBLE INTERFACING: 1 package (20″ × 45″), such as Shape-Flex (by C&T Publishing)

BATTING: 17½″ × 17½″

CUTTING

T-SHIRTS: Cut 4 squares 6″ × 6″, centering the designs or logos.

LIGHTWEIGHT FUSIBLE INTERFACING:
Cut 4 squares 6″ × 6″.

GRAY:
Cut 2 strips 2″ × width of fabric; from the strips cut:

- 4 strips 2″ × 7½″
- 4 strips 2″ × 6″

Cut 3 strips 1″ × width of fabric; from the strips cut:

- 2 strips 1″ × 17½″
- 2 strips 1″ × 16½″
- 4 strips 1″ × 6″
- 4 strips 1″ × 5½″

Cut 2 pieces 9″ × 17½″ for the backing.

BRIGHT COLORS:
Cut 1 strip of each color 1½″ × 18″ for the sashing.

Cut 1 strip 2″ × 20″ from each of 5 colors for the ties.

Construction

Seam allowances are ¼".

Block Centers

1. Following the manufacturer's instructions, iron the fusible interfacing to the back of the T-shirt squares.

2. Trim the squares to 5½" × 5½", keeping the design or logo centered.

Make the Colorful Sashing

1. Sew together the strips, following the diagram, or in any order you wish. Press all seams to one side.

2. Cross-cut this strip set into 10 strips 1½" wide.

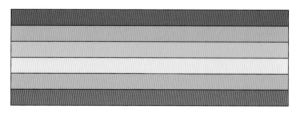

3. Add or remove squares to create 4 strips that are 7 squares (7½") long and 4 strips that are 8 squares (8½") long.

Tip

If you wish to duplicate the sashing in my sample, separate some of your strips and add some longer color sections.

Add the Sashing

Press toward the gray sashing after sewing each seam.

BLOCK 1

1. Sew a gray 1″ × 5½″ strip to the right side of the center block.

2. Sew a gray 1″ × 6″ strip to the bottom of the block.

3. Sew a gray 2″ × 6″ strip to the left side of the block.

4. Sew a gray 2″ × 7½″ strip to the top of the block.

5. Sew a colorful 1½″ × 7½″ strip to the right of the block.

6. Sew a colorful 1½″ × 8½″ strip to the bottom of the block.

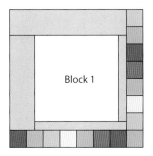

BLOCK 2

1. Sew a gray 1″ × 5½″ strip to the top of the center block.

2. Sew a gray 1″ × 6″ strip to the right side of the block.

3. Sew a gray 2″ × 6″ strip to the bottom of the block.

4. Sew a gray 2″ × 7½″ strip to the left side of the block.

5. Sew a colorful 1½″ × 7½″ strip to the top of the block.

6. Sew a colorful 1½″ × 8½″ strip to the right side of the block.

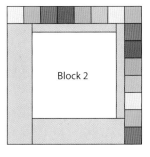

BLOCK 3

1. Sew a gray 1″ × 5½″ strip to the left side of the center block.

2. Sew a gray 1″ × 6″ strip to the bottom of the block.

3. Sew a gray 2″ × 6″ strip to the right side of the block.

4. Sew a gray 2″ × 7½″ strip to the top of the block.

5. Sew a colorful 1½″ × 7½″ strip to the left side of the block.

6. Sew a colorful 1½″ × 8½″ strip to the bottom of the block.

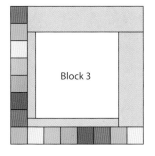

BLOCK 4

1. Sew a gray 1″ × 5½″ strip to the left side of the center block.

2. Sew a gray 1″ × 6″ strip to the top of the block.

3. Sew a gray 2″ × 6″ strip to the right side of the block.

4. Sew a gray 2″ × 7½″ strip to the bottom of the block.

5. Sew a colorful 1½″ × 7½″ strip to the left side of the block.

6. Sew a colorful 1½″ × 8½″ strip to the top of the block.

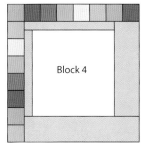

Make the Ties

1. Fold each tie in half lengthwise and press a crease.

2. Open and fold the long edges in to meet the center crease. Fold over again and press

3. Stitch down the center of each tie with a straight or decorative stitch.

4. Cut each tie in half to create 2 ties 10″ in length.

Put It Together

1. Sew together the blocks into 2 rows of 2 blocks. Press the seams in alternate directions so they nest when the rows are sewn together.

2. Sew together the rows. Press.

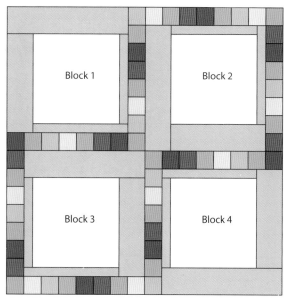

Block assembly

3. Add the 1″ × 16½″ narrow borders to the top and bottom. Press.

4. Add the 1″ × 17½″ narrow borders to the sides. Press.

5. Make the backing by sewing together the 2 backing pieces, leaving an 8″ opening in the center of the seam. Press.

Leave open for turning.

6. Evenly space each set of ties along the front top edge of the quilt, with the raw edges of the ties matching the raw top edge of quilt. Place the ties at least ¼″ in from the side seams. Baste the ties in place.

7. Place the quilt right side up on the batting. Place the backing on top of the quilt with right sides facing.

8. Stitch all the way around using a walking foot, if available. Trim the corners.

9. Turn the quilt right side out by pulling it through opening in backing. Carefully use the point of your scissors or the blunt end of another tool to poke out the corners crisply.

10. Hand stitch the opening in the backing closed.

11. Quilt as desired.

Birdies

Make the Birdies

1. Fuse the fabric to both sides of the fast2fuse for the birds and wings.

2. Trim the excess fabric and trim the wings down as desired to fit on the birds.

3. Freehand cut a beak for each bird, making the beak larger than necessary to make sure it gets stitched in when edgestitching the bird. Use glue or fusible web to hold it in place until it's time to stitch.

4. Stitch all around each bird ⅛˝ from the edge, making sure to stitch the beak.

5. Place a wing on each bird and zigzag all around each wing, attaching it to the bird.

6. Measure how long the pipe cleaners need to be to fit on your chosen hanging rod. Glue or stitch the pipe cleaners onto the back side of each bird.

7. Wrap pipe cleaners around the hanging rod to place the birds on their perch.

MATERIALS

COLORFUL SCRAPS

INTERFACING SCRAPS: Heavyweight double-sided fusible interfacing, such as fast2fuse HEAVY (by C&T Publishing)

BROWN PIPE CLEANERS: 2

CUTTING

COLORFUL SCRAPS: Using the bird patterns (pullout page P2), cut:

• 2 each of the larger Bird C and wing ¼˝ larger than the pattern

• 2 each of the smaller Bird D and wing ¼˝ larger than the pattern

FAST2FUSE: Using the bird patterns (pullout page P2), cut:

• 1 each of the larger Bird C and wing

• 1 each of the smaller Bird D and wing

More Little Gems from Joyce

For the *Oh Baby! Quilted Wallhanging*:

• Joyce suggested that you could use colors to match the baby's room or use lace from a handkerchief or wedding gown.

• This quilt would also be a great place to display Scout badges, sports ribbons, collectible pins, buttons, antique jewelry, and pins from special family members.

• Do you know about redwork embroidery? It's a wonderful vintage embroidery style using red thread, and it would look great in this project.

Wedding Memories Collage

Finished framed collage: 19″ × 23″

MATERIALS

PICTURE FRAME: Suggested size 19″ × 23″

FAMILY WEDDING PHOTOS

PRINTABLE FABRIC SHEETS: Available at most quilting or craft stores

SCRAPS OF FABRIC

BATTING: A piece slightly larger than the opening of your picture frame

TRIMS: Velvet ribbons, lace, fabric flowers, buttons, brooches, any trims you can dream up to use. This would be a great use for some of the old family costume jewelry you may never wear but would love to display.

As I sit here writing this book, our family is excitedly preparing for my sister's only son to get married in Chicago in a few weeks. Weddings are a big deal. It's not only the beginning of a new chapter in this young couple's life, but it's an expansion of our family tree and a new family being formed.

This child is my sister's firstborn. When she told me she was expecting, I was 16 years old and I burst into tears. Up to that point, I had always been the baby of the family. Silly and selfish, I know. When that sweet boy arrived, I couldn't get enough of him. I volunteered to babysit often and used to hold him and smell his cute little baby head. Now he is a college graduate, a successful businessman, and soon to be a husband. I imagine that in the not-too-distant future, he will be having babies of his own and I will once again burst into tears, and then treasure those fleeting moments of life when it's brand new.

Thinking about this new family beginning and reflecting back on my own heritage of love gives me a warm feeling of peace. I think when I created this Wedding Memories Collage I was hoping that I could capture some of those warm feelings in fabric and share them with the happy couple. This project lets you explore your creative side, with no right or wrong way of pulling it all together. Let your heart be your guide and create something lovely for the newlyweds using your memories of many loves in the family that have grown like theirs.

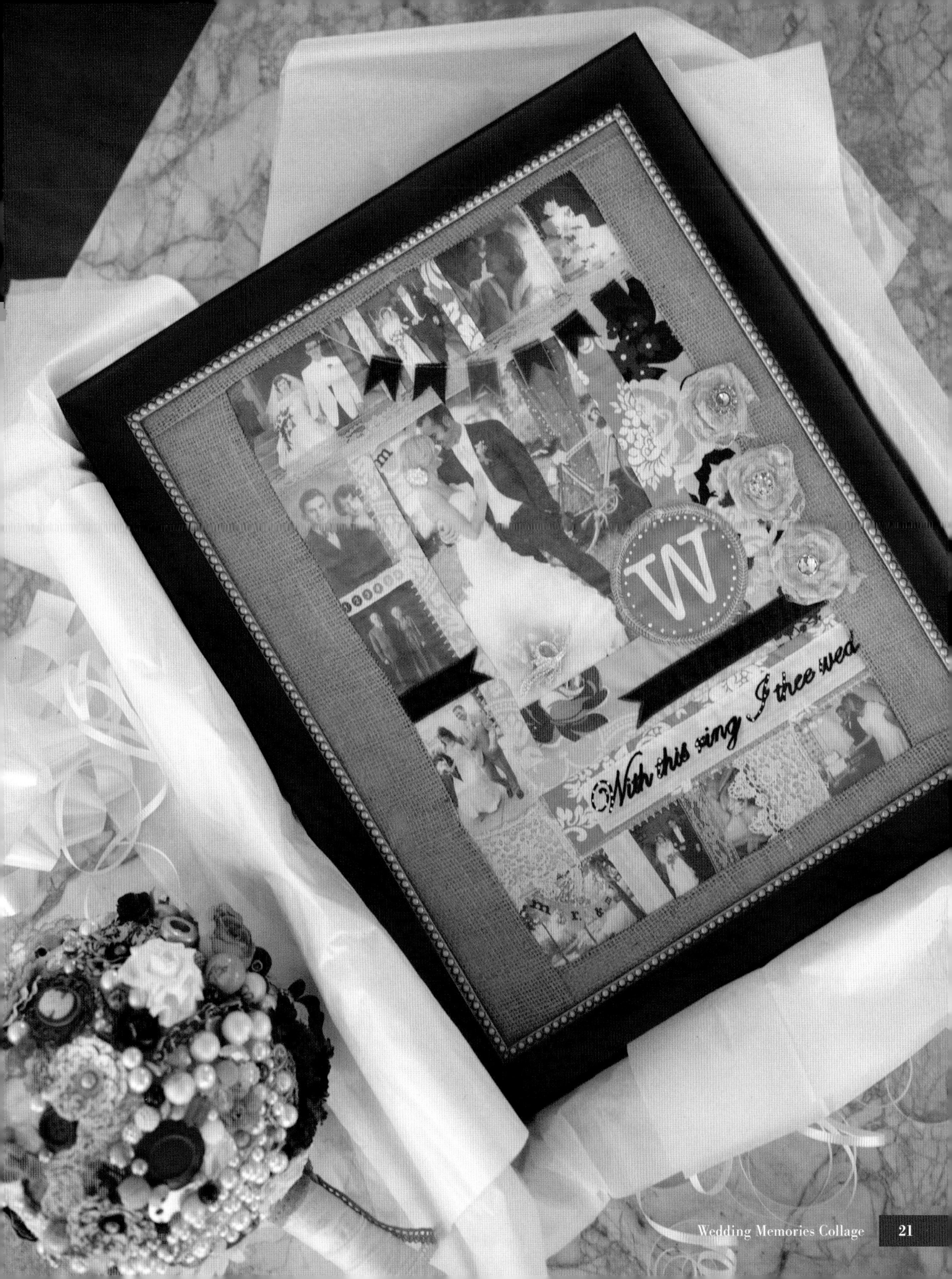
W
With this ring I thee wed

Tip

For best results, use photo-editing software to adjust your photos as needed.
Keep in mind that fabric absorbs some of the ink, so it's a good idea to
increase the saturation and print a test photo before you print all your photos.

Construction

Seam allowances are ¼".

1. Prepare and print your photos on the printable fabric sheets as follows:

- A large photo of the newlywed couple to use in the center, keeping your frame size in mind. My center photo is about 7" × 9" and my frame opening is 15½" × 19½".

- Photos from the wedding including parents, grandparents, siblings, and guests. Print them any size you like but keep them smaller than the center photo of the couple. The largest of mine is 3" × 4".

- Consider adding names, initials, wedding dates, and other meaningful text.

Note: *When printing photos, keep in mind that you will need a ¼" seam allowance around the perimeter of each picture. You will be creating a single block from these photos to fit inside the picture frame.*

2. Decide on an arrangement of photos to fill the picture frame, positioning all the pieces (photos, fabrics, large pieces of trim) before sewing anything together.

Note: *The finished block should be large enough to wrap around the frame backing (usually made of cardboard), but plan on having the batting the same size as the backing; otherwise, there will be too much bulk to fit the backing into the frame.*

3. Stitch together all the pieces, pressing the seams open as you go. If you prefer, you can topstitch the pieces together and cover the seams (or not) with trim.

4. Place the completed photo block on the batting and quilt as desired.

5. Let your creative spirit run free—embellish the photo block with ribbons, lace, buttons, paint, brooches, embroidery, or whatever comes to mind.

6. Wrap the quilted piece around the frame backing and secure the backing into the frame.

7. Write a lovely note on the back of the frame commemorating the event. Be sure to sign your name. This is a cherished piece of artwork that will surely be in their family for a long time to come.

Tip

This type of framed collage is also a great gift for other occasions such as milestone birthdays, graduations, anniversaries, and more.

Every Day Is a Celebration Dress

Finished dress: 3–6 months (fancy version),
6–12 months (casual version)

When my twin girls arrived, I was Super Mom in over-drive. I wanted to create special handmade dresses for them to wear at their christening that they could pass down to their children. The problem was, I didn't know how to sew garments. Heck, I was still learning how to sew. Our dear friend Auntie Irene helped me create exactly what I envisioned: a simple, sweet vintage-style gown (actually, for me it was gowns, because with twins everything is plural).

I love the satisfaction of quick results with my projects. What busy mom doesn't? This project embellishes an existing onesie into something amazing. Use layers of luxurious lace and a pretty sash for a stunning special-occasion dress (fancy version for sizes 3–6 months), or make it casual by using cottons and knits to make a color-ful everyday outfit (casual version for sizes 6–12 months).

Every Day Is a Celebration Dress was inspired by that nesting instinct to create something wonderful for a new baby. Whether you are a new mom (and new sewist) stitching for your little one or an experienced sewist making something for a dear friend, this little dress will surely make any day a celebration.

Fancy Version, Size 3–6 Months

This long version has three tiers of ruffles and is not suitable for babies who are walking, as this is a long dress that will reach their toes or beyond.

MATERIALS

LACE: 7 yards of lace trim, 6″ wide (or 4 yards of allover lace fabric; this length eliminates extra seams)

COTTON FABRIC: 1 yard to go under the lace

SASH FABRIC: 1⅔ yards sheer, chiffon-type fabric (⅜ yard of 60″ wide)

COTTON ONESIE

ELASTIC THREAD

ELASTIC: ¾ yard of ¼″ wide

CUTTING

LACE:
Cut 2 pieces 6″ × 72″ for Tiers 1 and 2.

Cut 1 piece 6″ × 108″ for Tier 3.

COTTON:
Cut 1 piece on the fold 6″ × 12″ for a total length of 6″ × 24″.

Cut 1 piece on the fold 6″ × 17″ for a total length of 6″ × 34″.

Cut 1 piece on the fold 6″ × 19″ for a total length of 6″ × 38″.

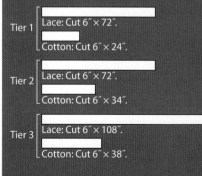

Tier 1 — Lace: Cut 6″ × 72″. Cotton: Cut 6″ × 24″.

Tier 2 — Lace: Cut 6″ × 72″. Cotton: Cut 6″ × 34″.

Tier 3 — Lace: Cut 6″ × 108″. Cotton: Cut 6″ × 38″.

SASH: Cut 1 piece 12″ × length of fabric (or across width if 60″ wide).

Construction

Seam allowances are ⅜″ unless otherwise noted.

Make the Skirt

1. For each cotton and lace band, with right sides facing, sew together the short edges and press seams to one side. Turn the bands right side out. Repeat for all 3 tiers.

2. Hem the bottom edge of the Tier 3 cotton by turning under ¼″ twice and stitching. Serge or zigzag stitch to finish the raw edges of all tiers.

3. Using a sewing machine with a gathering stitch, gather each lace band and baste to the coordinating tier. Finish raw edges with a zigzag stitch or a finish of your choice.

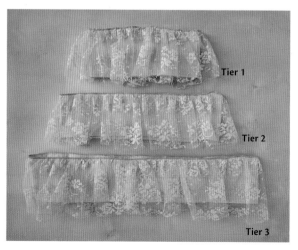

Tier 1

Tier 2

Tier 3

Tip

To gather without a gathering stitch, zigzag stitch over a length of buttonhole or heavy thread within the seam allowance, making sure not to stitch into the heavy thread. Mark the halfway and quarter-points of the lace and cotton tier with pins. Wrap one end of the heavy thread around a pin; then gently pull on the thread to gather each quarter section of lace to fit the cotton section, wrapping the thread around the pins to keep it gathered until you baste it. Baste the lace to the cotton tier, removing the pins, and then remove the heavy thread.

4. Gather Tier 2 along the top edge using elastic thread: Tie a knot in the end of the elastic thread; then zigzag stitch over the elastic thread ⅛″ from edge (making sure not to catch the elastic in the stitching), gently pulling as you sew all around the top of Tier 2 so it will match the width of Tier 1. Pull the elastic thread and adjust as needed.

5. With right sides facing, pin the top of Tier 2 to the bottom of cotton Tier 1, moving the Tier 1 lace aside to keep it free. Stitch the top of Tier 2 to the bottom of the Tier 1 cotton layer only, keeping the Tier 1 lace layer out of the seam. Remove the elastic thread.

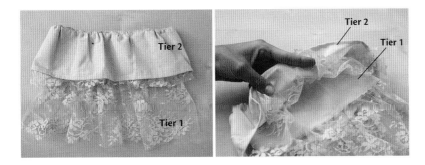

6. In the same manner, attach Tier 3 to Tier 2.

7. Measure the width of the onesie. Multiply that number by 2 and add ½″. Cut a piece of ¼″ elastic this length. Divide the elastic and the skirt top into quarters, and mark each quarter-point with a pin. Pin the elastic to the skirt top at those marks. Using a zigzag stitch, sew the elastic to the skirt, gently pulling the elastic as you sew all the way around. The pin markers help to evenly distribute the fabric gathers.

8. Use a ruler and pencil to lightly to mark a guideline 2″ below the arm hole. Using this line, place the *wrong* side of the skirt facing the *right* side of the onesie. Pin and use a zigzag stitch to sew the skirt to the onesie.

Make the Sash

1. Fold sash in half lengthwise, with right sides facing. Pin the sash along the long edge. Begin stitching at one short end and sew across at a 45° angle to create a nice angled end. Continue sewing the long edge until about the middle; then stop sewing and leave a 3″ opening for turning. Begin sewing the long edge again and continue to the opposite end, finishing with a 45° angle across the short edge.

2. Trim the angled seams, turn the sash right side out, and hand stitch the opening closed.

3. To create a bow in the front, off to one side, place the sash around the onesie so the ties are even and in the place where you want to tie it. Gently gather the sash along the side seams and pin. Stitch the sash down on the side seams. Gently gather the sash and tie a gorgeous bow or a simple knot, and you are all done!

Tip

Add embellishments at the neckline, if desired, such as a piece of lace gathered by hand and sewn in place.

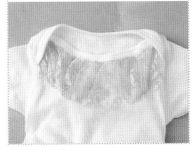

Construction

Seam allowances are ⅜″ unless otherwise noted.

1. With right sides facing, sew the short ends of the top skirt together. Repeat for the underskirt and the knit band.

2. Hem the top skirt and underskirt by turning under the bottom edges ¼″ twice and stitching. Serge or zigzag to finish the upper edges.

3. Layer the top skirt and underskirt together so that top raw edges match.

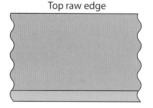

Top raw edge

4. Gather the skirts along the top edge using elastic thread in the same manner as in Make the Skirt, Step 4 (page 27).

5. With right sides facing, stitch the top of the skirts to the bottom of knit band using a zigzag stitch.

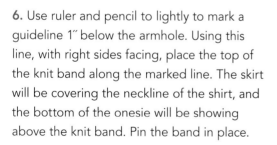

6. Use ruler and pencil to lightly to mark a guideline 1″ below the armhole. Using this line, with right sides facing, place the top of the knit band along the marked line. The skirt will be covering the neckline of the shirt, and the bottom of the onesie will be showing above the knit band. Pin the band in place.

7. Using a zigzag stitch, attach the skirt to the onesie or T-shirt, turn it right side out, and you're done!

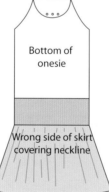

Bottom of onesie

Wrong side of skirt covering neckline

Place right side of knit band facing right side of onesie.

Casual Version, Size 6–12 Months

MATERIALS

JERSEY KNIT: ¼ yard for band

WOVEN COTTON: ¼ yard for top skirt

CONTRASTING WOVEN COTTON: ¼ yard for underskirt

COTTON ONESIE OR T-SHIRT

ELASTIC THREAD

CUTTING

JERSEY KNIT: Measure the width of the onesie or T-shirt. Multiply that number by 2 and add 2″. Cut a band 3½″ × this measurement.

TOP SKIRT: Cut 1 piece 7″ × width of fabric.

UNDERSKIRT: Cut 1 piece 8″ × width of fabric.

Happy Birthday Celebration Shirt

Two weeks before I turned sixteen, I found the prettiest pink dress at the store where I worked. I hung it in my closet and made sure it was nice and pressed. The morning of my sixteenth birthday, I couldn't wait to put it on. I wore it to school and I felt like a queen. It was always so much fun to wear something special for my birthday. Now that I am a couple of years older than sixteen (or a decade or so, whatever), I still like to wear something pretty on my birthday. Only now, that usually involves a new pair of adorable pajama pants and extra-fuzzy socks. That might be a story for another day, though.

One of the joys of having kids, grandkids, nieces, and nephews of your own is making them something special to wear on their special day. These two adorable appliqués are perfect for a special day, whether that special someone is turning 6, 16, or even 36. I have even made these shirts as favors for my girls' birthday parties. Add an initial instead of a number and you have a great, everyday, special shirt.

MATERIALS

ASSORTED FAT QUARTERS OR SCRAPS:
- 2 colors for the pirate octopus and scarf
- 4 colors for the cake, stand, and candles

YELLOW: small scrap for the candle flames

BLACK FELT: small square or scrap for octopus eye patch

TAN FELT: small square or scrap for octopus eye

COTTON T-SHIRT

PAPER-BACKED FUSIBLE WEB: or use Wash-Away Appliqué Sheets (by C&T Publishing)

WASHABLE GLUE (optional)

CUTTING

To cut out and prepare the appliqué pieces, refer to A Few Words about Appliqué (page 110) and appliqué patterns (pullout page P1).

Note: Create the number appliqué pattern using the font of your choice, printing it out so that it is 2˝ tall.

CAKE:
Cut candle flames.

Cut 1 cake stand.

Cut 1 strip 1½˝ × 14˝ for cake top ruffle.

Cut 3 strips 1˝ × 6½˝ for horizontal strips of basket weave.

Cut 6 strips 1˝ × 3˝ for vertical strips of basket weave.

Cut 1 strip 1˝ × 7˝ for cake bottom trim.

Cut ⅛˝ × 2½˝ strips for candles.

OCTOPUS PIRATE:
Cut 1 octopus.

Cut 1 eye patch.

Cut 1 scarf.

Cut 1 eye.

Construction

Preparation

1. Preshrink the T-shirt by washing and drying it. Press any wrinkles out of the appliqué area.

2. Cut out and prepare the appliqué shapes for the T-shirt(s) you plan to make. Use the appliqué method of your choice to sew down the appliqué pieces in the order below.

Cake Shirt

1. Arrange all the appliqué pieces on the T-shirt to determine the placement.

2. Pin down the cake stand and appliqué it in place.

3. Place the 3 horizontal basket weave pieces so the bottom piece touches the top of the cake stand. Weave the 6 vertical pieces into place. Use pins, fusible web, or washable glue to hold the cake together.

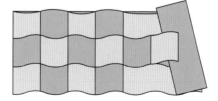

Tip

For the candle flames and eye of the octopus, you can freehand cut the pieces, using the patterns as a guide.

4. Stitch the cake block in place using a straight stitch, stitching an outside rectangle and then 2 inner rectangles.

5. For the bottom cake trim, press under the short ends ¼˝; then press under the long edges ¼˝ on each side. Place the trim overlapping the bottom of the basket weave block and slightly over the cake stand. Stitch it in place using a straight stitch.

6. If you are using a number, stitch it in place now.

7. To make the top of the cake, use a gathering stitch (see Tip, page 26) down the center of the cake top ruffle strip and gather it to the same width as cake. Place it on top of the cake but do not pin in place yet.

8. Place candles as desired, tucking the ends under the ruffle strip. After the candles are placed, set the ruffle strip aside and sew the candles in place. Sew the flames above the candles.

9. Turn under the short ends of the ruffle strip and pin the ruffle strip slightly overlapping the top of the cake. The long edges of the ruffle are left raw and will fray slightly with washings, which will give it a fluffy, soft look. (Hem the long edges if you prefer a more finished look.)

10. Stitch the ruffle in place.

Gift this shirt to your favorite birthday girl!

Octopus Shirt

1. Arrange all the appliqué pieces on the T-shirt to determine the placement. The octopus is designed to be placed more toward the right side of shirt, with 3 of the tentacles running to the side seam of the shirt.

2. Pin down the octopus tentacles and appliqué them in place.

Tip

You may find it helpful to use basting glue to hold the tentacles in place while you sew them down.

3. Place the scarf on the octopus head.

4. Appliqué the octopus head and scarf in place.

5. Appliqué the eye patch and eye in place.

6. Stitch an eyeball on the eye by hand or machine.

7. Using a marking pen, mark a smile on the octopus. Use a tight zigzag or satin stitch to stitch the smile. **Note:** *Practice on a scrap piece of fabric to get the stitch size correct.*

8. If you are using a number, stitch it in place now.

Gift this shirt to your favorite birthday boy!

Tip

Add an initial or appliqué a name to either shirt to make it an everyday-is-awesome kind of shirt.

Twice as Nice Bow Tie

Being the mom of twins, I'm not gonna lie: I have always loved dressing our babies alike. Our twins are the cutest little identical girls ever, and since I'm their mom, I'm allowed to be biased like that. Whenever we get stopped with our girls and someone asks, "Are they twins?" my husband's favorite response is, "No, they are triplets. We left the other one at home." I roll my eyes at him and then smile at the person and respond yes. Twins and triplets run in our family, so when my niece had boy/girl twins a few years ago, it was only natural to come up with a cute way to coordinate their outfits.

This sweet little project makes the perfect gift for coordinating siblings—a bow tie for him, and a headband with matching bow tie for her. This would also be adorable to coordinate for a mom and her son.

Boy's Bow Tie

MATERIALS

COTTON: 1 fat quarter (18″ × 22″) for tie

LIGHTWEIGHT FUSIBLE INTERFACING: ¼ yard, such as Shape-Flex

BOW-TIE HARDWARE: 2 alligator clips or bar-pin back (For bow-tie hardware, see Resources, page 111.)

HOT-GLUE GUN (optional)

CUTTING

TIE FABRIC:
Cut 1 rectangle 4″ × 10″.

Cut 1 square 2½″ × 2½″.

INTERFACING:
Cut 1 rectangle 4″ × 10″.

Cut 1 square 2½″ × 2½″.

Twins run in our family. This is my great niece and nephew, Autumn and Aiden.

Construction

Seam allowances are ¼".

1. Following the manufacturer's instructions, fuse the interfacing to the wrong side of the corresponding fabric pieces.

2. Fold the 4″ × 10″ rectangle in half lengthwise, with rights sides facing, and sew the long side to create a tube. Turn the tube right side out.

3. Center the seam and press. The side with the seam is the back.

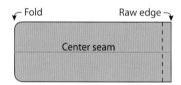

Fold   Raw edge

Center seam

4. With the seam side out, fold the tube in half crosswise and sew the short edges together with a zigzag stitch to create a tube with finished edges. Turn the tube right side out with the new seam at the center back. Set aside.

Tip

Use a safety pin to help turn this small tube. Place the pin as shown; then thread it through the tube and gently turn the tube right side out.

5. Repeat Steps 2–4 with the 2½″ × 2½″ square.

6. Pinch the larger tube into an M shape and thread it through the small tube, pulling the small tube to the center of the bow. Tack in place.

7. Attach the hardware to the back of the tie using hot glue or stitch in place. If you're using alligator clips, glue with the teeth facing out so you can clip them to each side of the collar.

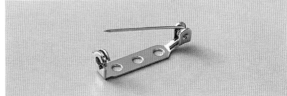

Bar-pin back

Two alligator clips

Construction

Seam allowances are ¼˝. Follow the construction of Boy's Bow Tie, Steps 2–6 (pages 36 and 37), to create the headband bow.

Make the Ruffle

When making the ruffle, use an unfinished edge for a more vintage look or a finished edge for a more polished look.

- *For the vintage look:*

    Cut 1 rectangle 2˝ × 12˝ from the ruffle fabric.

- *For the more polished look:*

    Cut 1 rectangle 3˝ × 13˝ from the ruffle fabric.

    Press under ¼˝ along the short edges.

    Press under ½˝ along the long edges.

    Stitch around all 4 sides to secure these edges.

Girl's Bow Headband

MATERIALS

COTTON: 1 fat quarter (18˝ × 22˝) for bow

COORDINATING COTTON: 1 fat quarter for ruffle

LACE TRIM: such as ¾˝-wide lace hem tape

FELT: 1 piece 9˝ × 12˝ in a complementary color

HEADBAND: I love the Goody brand girls' fabric-covered headbands—they are soft to wear.

HOT-GLUE GUN

CUTTING

BOW FABRIC:
Cut 1 rectangle 3˝ × 9˝.

Cut 1 square 2½˝ × 2½˝.

FELT: Cut 1 rectangle 1˝ × 4˝.

Put It Together

1. Stitch a gathering stitch (see Tip, page 26) down the long center of the strip.

2. Gather the strip evenly until it measures 4″.

3. Measure and mark 2″ up from one end on the headband.

4. Glue the felt to the underside of the headband with one edge at the 2″ mark.

5. Glue the ruffle to the top side of the felt and the headband. Press and hold until the glue cools.

6. Glue the lace trim on the center of the ruffle, covering the gathering stitch.

7. Glue the bow in place.

Sewing Kit

Finished kit: 10″ × 8″ (folded), 30″ × 24″ (unfolded)

Never wanting to force my love of sewing on my own children, I gently introduced my fabric and thread obsession over time. (Okay, there may have been a little bit of coercion or perhaps some minor bribery involved. Whatever.) First, there was a little pillow. Then my mother made a doll quilt with each of them. And the next thing I knew, my girls were sewing up the most amazing dresses for a 4-H county fair project. I had visions the three of them taking over the Two Peas corporation (a.k.a. my sewing room) one day. And then it happened. They developed their own opinions and desires. Huh. Fancy that.

One of my Peas *loves* sewing, and she is quite good. She is also too much like me because she does her own thing and won't take a lick of instruction from me. The other Pea can take sewing or leave it. She's my gymnast and would rather be outside turning cartwheels. I imagine someday she'll come back to sewing. And Sprout, my youngest, has sat on my lap while I sew away in the afternoons since she was born. To this day, she still loves to sit with me while I sew. I love that time with her.

MATERIALS

LINEN-LOOK CANVAS: 1 yard for exterior, 2 interior panels, and pocket

COTTON PRINTS OR SOLIDS: 5 fat quarters for interior decorative patchwork plus ½ yard

SCRAPS FOR APPLIQUÉ

LIGHTWEIGHT FUSIBLE INTERFACING: 2 packages (each 20″ × 45″), such as Shape-Flex

MEDIUM-WEIGHT FUSIBLE FLEECE INTERFACING: ¼ yard

ZIPPER: 12″ length (nylon, *not* metal)

BUTTON: 1 (¾″ wide)

ELASTIC: 10″ length of ½″ wide

FELT: Scrap, at least 1¾″ × 2″ for needle holder

CUTTING

As you cut, I suggest that you label each piece. Follow my design, or mix and match your fabrics however you like.

COTTON PRINTS OR SOLIDS:
Cut 4 pieces 2½″ × 10½″ for left panel.

Cut 2 pieces 5½″ × 10½″ for center panel pocket.

Cut 1 piece 1½″ × 10½″ for center panel zipper trim.

Cut 1 piece 8½″ × 10½″ for right panel.

Cut 2 pieces 6½″ × 10½″ for right panel pocket.

Cut 2 pieces 4″ × 9½″ for right panel pocket flap.

Cut 4 pieces 3″ × 8½″ for bottom panel.

Cut 1 piece 2″ × 15″ for elastic cover.

Cut 2 strips 2″ × 28″ for ties.

CUTTING continued on page 42

LINEN-LOOK CANVAS:

Cut 1 piece 8½″ × 10½″ for center panel.

Cut 1 piece 8½″ × 10½″ for top panel.

Cut 1 piece 5″ × 10″ for top panel tools pocket.

Cut 1 piece for cross-shaped exterior after you have completed the interior panel.

LIGHTWEIGHT INTERFACING:

Cut 5 pieces 8½″ × 10½″ for left, center, right, top, and bottom panels.

Cut 1 piece 5½″ × 10½″ for center panel pocket.

Cut 1 piece 6½″ × 10½″ for right panel pocket.

Cut 1 piece 4″ × 9½″ for the right panel pocket flap.

FLEECE INTERFACING:

Cut 1 piece 5″ × 10″ for center panel pocket.

Cut 1 piece 6″ × 10″ for right panel pocket.

Cut 1 piece 3½″ × 9″ for right panel pocket flap.

Since one of the Peas attends sewing workshops through her 4-H club, I was inspired to make her a little sewing kit travel bag for all her gear. It's got pockets and zippers and sweet little stitching. You can choose different pocket options, and add or omit pockets or other aspects of the kit to fit your needs. I think even grown-up girls will enjoy this project. You will love making this for any of your sewing friends, big or small.

Sprout has confiscated this project, not for sewing but for filling with her toys and art supplies. This little kit can have multiple purposes beyond sewing, so be creative with how you use it.

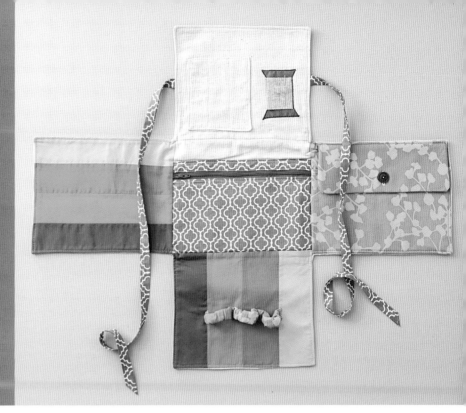

Construction

*Seam allowances are ¼˝
unless otherwise noted.*

Interior

LEFT PANEL

1. Sew together the 4 strips of the left panel along the long edges. Press the seams open.

2. Fuse the lightweight interfacing onto the wrong side of the panel and set it aside.

CENTER PANEL WITH ZIP POCKET

1. Fuse the lightweight interfacing onto the wrong side of the panel.

2. On one pocket piece, fuse the fleece interfacing to the wrong side, matching one long edge and centering it between the short sides. On the other pocket piece, fuse the lightweight interfacing.

3. Place the interfaced pocket panel piece with the fabric side up, Place the closed zipper faceup along the top edge, with the zipper pull to the right. Place the remaining fleece-lined pocket panel on top, wrong side up and with the unlined edge at the top, making a zipper sandwich. Pin together and then sew ¼˝ away from the edge of the zipper teeth.

Note: *If you have a zipper foot, use it for this step. If you do not have a zipper foot, adjust the needle position to the left or right to make this step easier.*

4. Turn right side out and press the seam with wrong sides together. Topstitch along the seam.

5. Press under ⅜″ of the long edges of the center panel zipper trim so it is ¾″ wide.

6. Pin the center pocket onto center panel, matching the raw edges at the bottom. Place the zipper trim over the top of the zipper, ¼″ from the zipper teeth. Pin together and then topstitch along the zipper trim top and bottom ⅛″ from the edge.

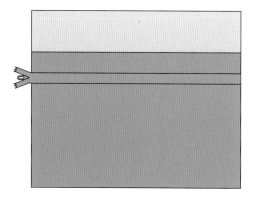

RIGHT PANEL WITH DIVIDED POCKET WITH A FLAP

1. Center and fuse the fleece interfacing to the wrong side of one of the pocket pieces and one of the flap pieces. Fuse the lightweight interfacing to the wrong sides of the panel, and the remaining pocket and flap pieces.

2. With right sides facing, pin together the pocket pieces. Sew along just the top edge.

3. Turn the pocket right side out, press, and topstitch the pocket piece along the top edge with 2 rows of topstitching.

4. Place the pocket on the main right panel, lining up the bottom edges. Pin the pocket in place. Divide the pocket as desired into 2 or 3 sections and mark the divisions with pins.

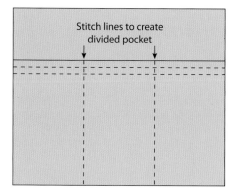

5. Sew along the marked lines on the pocket to attach it to the panel.

6. With right sides facing, pin together the flap pieces. Sew around the edges, leaving the top open. Gently round the corners as you sew.

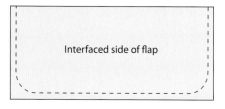

7. Clip the curves of the flap, turn them right side out, and press. Topstitch along the sewn edges.

8. Find the center and sew a 1″ buttonhole in the flap at the center, ½″ up from the bottom edge.

Buttonhole centered and ½″ from edge

9. Set aside the flap.

TOP PANEL WITH MINI-TOOLS POCKET

1. Fuse the lightweight interfacing to the wrong side of the top panel.

2. Fold the top panel tools pocket in half, right sides facing, to create a 5″ × 5″ square. Stitch around the edges, leaving a 2″ opening in the bottom for turning. Clip the corners.

3. Turn the pocket right side out and press, folding in the bottom edge opening. Topstitch along the top of the pocket.

4. Pin the pocket onto the left side of the top panel about 1″ away from the bottom and left edges, making sure there is room to fit the spool appliqué on this panel as well.

Tip

Use a spool of thread to mark the curves on the pocket flap if you need a guideline.

5. Divide the pocket as desired; mark and stitch along the marked lines to attach it to the panel. Stitch along the sides and bottom of the pocket. In the sample, 2 lines of stitching created 3 pockets for tools such as marking pens, a small ruler, and a seam ripper.

6. Using the spool pattern (page 49), cut out the spool. (Refer to A Few Words about Appliqué, page 110.)

7. Cut a piece of felt 1¾″ × 2″ to fit the center of the spool appliqué. Pin the spool and felt to the top panel and stitch in place, catching only one side of the felt square. Leave one side of the felt unsewn for access to stored needles.

BOTTOM PANEL WITH SPOOLS HOLDER

1. Sew together the 4 strips of the bottom panel along the long edges. Press the seams open.

2. Fuse the lightweight interfacing onto the wrong side of the panel and set it aside.

3. Fold the elastic cover fabric in half, right sides together, so it measures 1″ wide. Pin and then sew along the long edge, creating a tube.

4. Turn the tube right side out and press, with the seam down the center of one side.

5. Thread the elastic through the tube. When elastic reaches the end, pin through both the tube and elastic about 1″ from the end. Fold under the edge of the tube and stitch across the end to secure the elastic in place. Repeat on opposite end, pinning to keep the gathers out of the way.

6. Use a spool of your favorite brand of thread to determine the size of the loops needed to hold your spools. Mark 4 dots on the lower center panel to indicate each end and the stitching points.

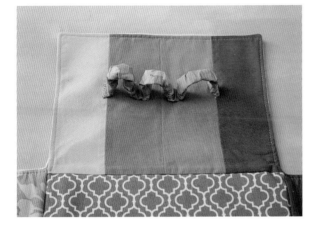

7. Pin the elastic band at the dots and stitch securely.

Put It Together

1. With right sides facing, place the top panel on the center panel, joining the top edge of the center panel and bottom edge of the top panel. Pin and sew. Press the seams to the top panel.

2. In a similar manner, add the right, left, and bottom panels to the center panel, pressing all seams away from the center panel. Refer to the kit photo to check placement.

3. Center the pocket flap to the top of the right panel. Pin and then baste it in place. Using the buttonhole as a guide, attach the button to the pocket.

4. With right sides facing, place the completed interior panel on the exterior fabric. Using the interior panel as your pattern, cut the exterior to match the interior.

5. Cut a piece of lightweight interfacing the same size as the exterior and fuse it to the wrong side of the exterior. You will need to fuse 2 pieces together to get the full width. Just cut an extra ½˝ on each piece and overlap them when fusing to the fabric.

6. Cut out the spool and hearts using the patterns (page 49) and prepare the appliqué. (Refer to A Few Words about Appliqué, page 110.)

7. Place the prepared appliqué on the exterior as shown. Edgestitch the appliqué to the exterior. Pay close attention to the orientation to be sure it shows correctly when the kit is closed. Using an erasable pen or pencil, write the words "love you sew" between the hearts. Set the stitch length to 3.5 and free-hand machine stitch the wording.

8. Create the ties: Fold the corners in to the center and press a point at one end of each tie; then fold and press ¼″ down each long edge. Press each tie in half and stitch closed.

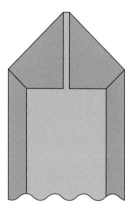

9. Center the ties with the raw edges matching, along the side of the front cover with the appliqué. Baste the ties in place. Pin the ties back inside the exterior to keep them out of the seam for the next step.

10. With right sides facing, pin the exterior and interior together. Note the orientation of each panel. Stitch the exterior and interior panels together, leaving a 6″ opening on one side for turning. Clip the inside and outside corners.

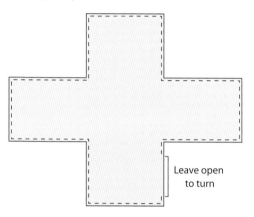

Leave open to turn

11. Turn the sewing kit right side out. Press; then topstitch ⅛″ from edge all around.

12. To close the kit, wrap ties to the back and cross, bring to the front, and tie in a bow.

Fill your sewing kit with your favorite sewing tools and head off to the local quilt shop for a class!

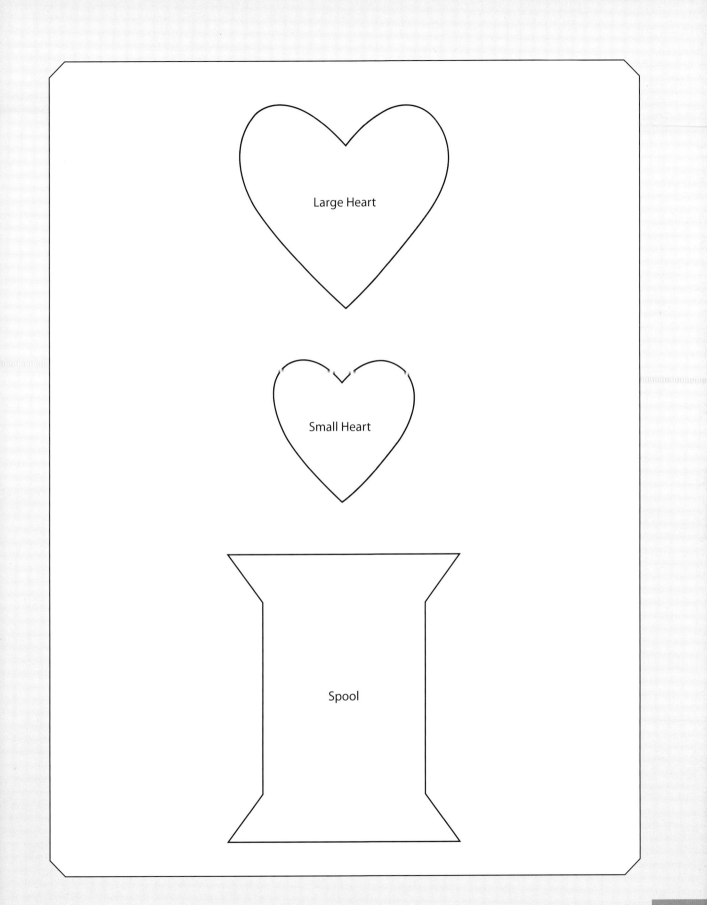

Large Heart

Small Heart

Spool

Recipe Binder Cover

Finished cover: 21¾″ × 12½″

So the story goes like this.

Me: "Mmm! Mom, how do you make your pumpkin pie?"

Mom: "I just follow the recipe on the side of the can."

(*Flash forward to a family dinner where I serve my "mother's pumpkin pie."*)

Me: "Mom, what did I do wrong? This doesn't taste like your pie."

Mom: "Did you follow the recipe on the can like I said? Did you add in a little of 'this' and a little of 'that'? That's how I make it."

Me: "Um, no, Mom. I followed the recipe on the side of the can, like you said."

Mom: "Oh, well, I just use that as my base and then add in my own stuff."

Sound all too familiar? Here's my advice. Have your mother actually write out her recipes. Make this super-cute cover for your binder and store those precious memories inside, including recipes from the side of a can. Good luck!

You can also use this for a scrapbook cover or for a school notebook—have fun with it and make it fit your very special purpose.

MATERIALS

SOLID LINEN: ½ yard for exterior and end pockets

COTTON PRINT: ½ yard for lining

FELT: 1 piece 9″ × 12″ of black

LIGHTWEIGHT FUSIBLE INTERFACING: 1 package (20″ × 45″), such as Shape-Flex

MEDIUM-WEIGHT FUSIBLE FLEECE: ½ yard

RIBBON: 16″ of 1½″ wide for bookmark

WAX PAPER OR OTHER TRACING PAPER

FUSIBLE WEB

BINDER: 10″ × 11½″ with ½″ rings

Tip

If you wish to use a binder with larger rings, measure the full width (front, spine, and back). Cut the exterior and lining to this measurement plus 1½″, and cut the interfacing and fleece to this measurement plus 1″.

CUTTING

SOLID LINEN:
Cut 1 piece 13½″ × 22½″ for exterior.

Cut 2 pieces 13½″ × 9½″ for inside pocket ends.

COTTON PRINT: Cut 1 piece 13½″ × 22½″ for lining.

SHAPE-FLEX: Cut 1 piece 13″ × 22″ for lining.

MEDIUM-WEIGHT FUSIBLE FLEECE: Cut 1 piece 13″ × 22″ for exterior.

Cut 2 pieces 7″ × 12½″ for pockets.

Construction

Seam allowances are ⅜˝.

Prepare the Appliqués

1. Using wax paper or other tracing paper, trace the whisk (page 55), each letter inside of the circle, and the circle.

2. Pin the traced designs onto the black felt.

3. Cut out whisk handle, circles, and the letters.

Tip

A nice, small pair of snips works great for fussy cutting the letters.

Make the Pockets

1. Press under ¼″ along the long side of the pocket pieces. Then press under again 2″ to create the finished edge.

2. Open the 2″ fold and place the medium-weight fusible fleece on the wrong side of the pocket next to this fold line, centered between the top and bottom. Fuse the fleece in place.

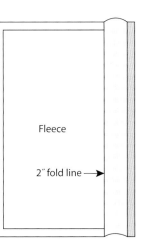

Fleece

2″ fold line →

3. Sew ¼″ from the folded edge to secure the interfacing in place. For an interesting detail, continue sewing lines ¼″ apart until you reach the edge of the folded piece.

Make the Cover

1. Center the Shape-Flex interfacing on the wrong side of the lining and fuse it in place, following the manufacturer's instructions.

2. Center the medium-weight fusible fleece on the exterior and fuse it in place, following the manufacturer's instructions.

3. To find the center for the appliqué placement, with the exterior panel right side up, measure and mark 7″ up on the right edge of the panel. Then measure left toward the center 5¼″ and mark. This should be close to the center of the front of your cover. Double-check to make sure it looks correct.

Make a Personalized Tag

Here's an easy way to make a personalized tag for your special book cover.

1. Download the free handmade book tag from my website (see Resources, page 111).

2. Open the tag in a photo-editing program and customize the text to include the date and your name.

3. Flip the tag to a reverse (mirror) image. Using Lesley Riley's TAP Transfer Artist Paper (by C&T Publishing), print the tag using an ink-jet printer.

4. Following the instructions on the TAP package, transfer the image to a square of the exterior fabric large enough to fit the image.

5. Sew the tag as desired on one of the inside pocket pieces.

4. Make several small holes in the traced whisk pattern along the wire lines. Place the pattern so that the lines end about ¼″ below the center so that you can cover up the ends with the felt whisk handle. Mark

Begin stitching ¼″ below the center point

pencil dots at these holes to outline the wires onto your fabric; then connect the dots with a light pencil line. Using black thread and a stitch length of around 4.0, stitch the wire lines.

5. Pin the whisk handle in place. Using white thread and a stitch length of around 4.0, stitch the handle in place.

6. Center the circles/letter appliqué just under the whisk and pin. Using white thread, stitch the appliqué in place. Don't forget the centers of the *e* and the *a*.

Put It Together

1. Place the exterior panel piece right side up. Measure 7″ from the left of the panel and place the ribbon right side down at this mark, with the raw edges matching at the top, and pin it in place.

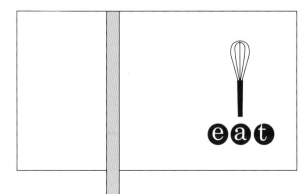

2. With right sides facing, place the 2 inside end pocket pieces in place with folded edges toward the center and pin.

3. Place the lining on top with right side down and pin. Using a ⅜″ seam, sew all around, leaving a 5″ opening in the bottom center for turning. Trim all 4 corners to reduce bulk.

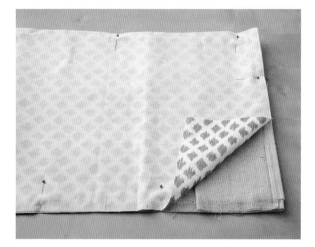

4. Turn the cover right side out. Carefully use the point of your scissors or the blunt end of another tool to poke out the corners crisply.

5. Press all the edges.

6. Use a small piece of fusible web to seal the open seam closed and then insert a binder.

Fill your binder with great recipes and memories from friends and family and pass it on to someone you love! (For free printable recipe cards, see Resources, page 111.)

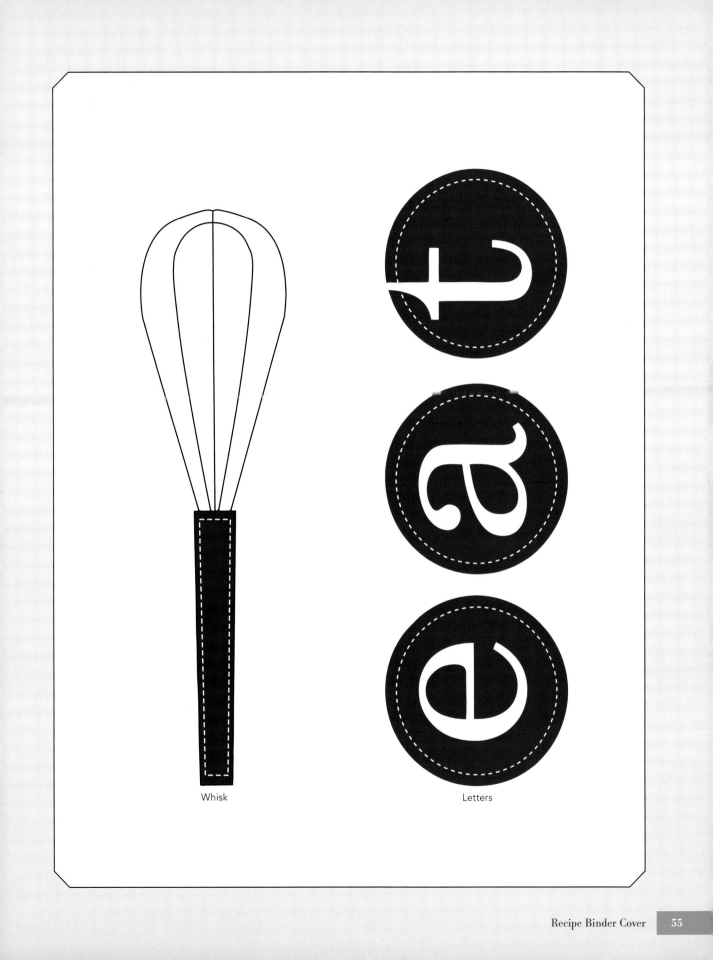

Whisk

Letters

Travel Pouches

Finished pouch: 6½″ × 4½″ (large), 3¼″ × 2¾″ (small)

These travel pouches are truly inspired: Inspired by sandy shorelines. Inspired by bike rides chasing after a rising tide. Inspired by warm ocean breezes on my skin that, when I close my eyes, make me feel like I'm in heaven. Inspired by traveling with my family to places where we can be quiet together, walk together, play together, and enjoy a little escape from the everyday hustle and bustle.

Organization is one thing that makes packing for these little adventures so much more enjoyable. The bigger travel pouch will hold the charging cords for your electronic devices, and the little pouch is perfect for your camera memory cards or extra battery. This little wallet can help you stay organized in a lot of different ways.

It's the perfect gift for just about everybody. Okay, maybe not absolutely everybody—my husband is not much for ruffles—but you get the idea. (Wink!)

MATERIALS

EXTERIOR: 1 fat quarter

LINING: 1 fat quarter (Note that this is the trim that shows on the exterior.)

HEAVYWEIGHT FUSIBLE FLEECE INTERFACING: ¼ yard, such as Pellon 971F

MAGNETIC SNAP: 1

RIBBON: 14″ length (*optional*)

CUTTING

See the patterns (pullout pages P1 and P2) for this project. Note the orientation of the pattern pieces for the exterior and lining. Place the pattern pieces on the right side of the fabric with the pattern right side up as noted.

EXTERIOR: Cut 1 from exterior pattern.

LINING:
Cut 1 from lining pattern.

Cut 1 strip 4″ × 22″ and 1 strip 4″ × 11″. With right sides facing, piece together the strips to make 1 long strip for the pleated strip.

INTERFACING:
Cut 1 from exterior pattern, following inner line.

Cut 1 from lining pattern, following inner line.

Construction

Seam allowances are ⅜″
unless otherwise noted.

1. Center and fuse the interfacing to the exterior and lining, following the manufacturer's instructions.

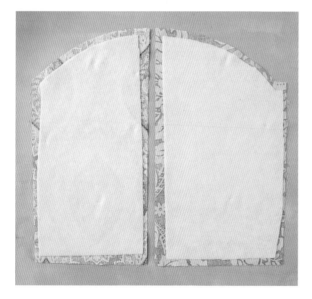

2. With right sides facing, fold the pleat strip in half lengthwise. Pin and sew, using a ¼″ seam, to create a long tube. Trim the seam allowance to ⅛″. Turn the tube right side out and press.

3. Create a box pleat (or use a gathering stitch to create a simple ruffle if you prefer). The box pleat used in this sample is 1″ wide and then folded under ¼″. Press the pleat.

4. Place the pleat strip 1½″ from the longer edge on the exterior panel. Add the ribbon, if desired, along the pleat seam. Sew to the exterior.

5. With right sides facing, pin the exterior and the lining together along the right edge. Sew.

6. Line up the lining and exterior on the left side. Pin and sew just the straight edge, not along the curve. Both ends should be open.

7. Flatten the pouch evenly. A small fold will be on each side of the lining; be sure these folds are even. Pin and sew along the top curve and along the bottom, leaving a 3″ opening in the center of the bottom for turning.

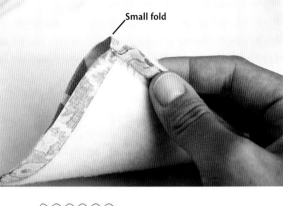

Small fold

Small folds

8. Clip the curved edge and turn the pouch right side out. Gently push out the corners and press along the seams. Be sure that the lining is showing evenly on each side of the front.

9. To attach the first half of the magnetic snap, find the center along the straight bottom edge and measure up 1¾″. Attach a half of the magnetic snap at this point, following the manufacturer's instructions.

10. Measure up 4″ from the straight bottom and mark. This is your fold line to form the pouch. Fold at this mark, pin, and press.

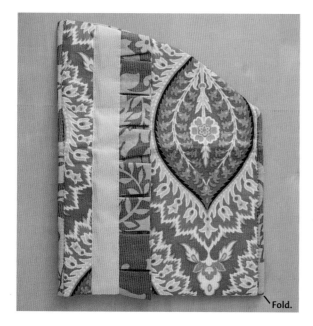

Fold.

12. Unpin the pouch at the fold, now that the magnetic snap is fully inserted. Press the open seam closed and topstitch across the straight edge ⅛″ from the edge.

13. Refold the pouch and pin the edges together. Using a stitch length of at least 3.5, carefully stitch in-the-ditch of the seam where the lining and exterior fabrics meet along the edges, completing the pouch.

Stitch in-the-ditch.

11. To attach the other half of the magnetic snap, find the center along the curved edge of the flap, measure down 1″, and mark. Fold the curved edge down and make sure that this mark matches with the magnetic snap in the lower portion of the pouch. Attach the snap. You will need to reach inside the pouch from the bottom opening to complete this task.

Tips

- *Stitch back and forth at the stress points at the top of the pouch pocket opening.*

- *Sew with the pleated trim and flap side up—this will help make sure that you are sewing in the seamline where you most often will see the stitching. If you sew with the pocket facing up, you may miss the seamline along the flap as that is not visible from that side.*

Small Pouch

1. With right sides facing, pin and sew together the exterior and lining, leaving the straight bottom edge open.

2. Clip the curved edge and turn the pouch right side out. Press.

3. Press in the open edge and topstitch the opening closed ⅛″ from the edge.

4. Fold up the bottom edge 2½″ and pin in place.

5. Start at one corner and topstitch ⅛″ from the edge down the side and around the curved flap to the other corner.

6. For the buttonhole, find the center of the curved flap and sew the buttonhole ½″ from the edge.

7. Sew on the button opposite the buttonhole.

MATERIALS

EXTERIOR: 1 fat quarter

LINING: 1 fat quarter

BUTTON: ½″ wide

CUTTING

See the patterns (pullout page P2) for this project.

EXTERIOR: Cut 1 from the small pouch pattern.

LINING: Cut 1 from the small pouch pattern.

Bicycle Basket

Finished basket: 9¼″ wide × 8″ tall × 4″ deep

I don't care if you are 4 or 40, getting a new bike is exciting. When our twins turned 4, we purchased them the cutest matching pink bikes with training wheels. And like most 4-year-olds, they had about a bazillion (because bazillion is an actual number in mom-world when referring to your kids' toys) teeny tiny toys that they had to carry with them everywhere they went.

The perfect accessory for bike-loving kids is a basket to carry all their bazillion toys. That love of bikes and baskets and carrying toys doesn't go away as you get older. The evidence is pictured here. This adorable turquoise bike belongs to our photographer, Britt. Britt loves to ride this down to the farmers' market and load up. I know that this basket will be the perfect gift for anyone 4, 40, or any age.

MATERIALS

COTTON PRINT: 1 yard for base, lining, and ties

COORDINATING COTTON PRINT: ½ yard for covered rope top of basket

COTTON CORDING: 12 yards of ¼″ laundry line or 8/32″ piping cord (such as Simplicity brand)

HEAVYWEIGHT FUSIBLE FLEECE INTERFACING: ½ yard, such as Pellon 971F

LIGHTWEIGHT FUSIBLE INTERFACING: 1 package (20″ × 45″), such as Shape-Flex

COTTON SCRAPS, TWINE, AND GREEN FELT: for embellishing

ZIPPER FOOT: to make and attach the cording (optional)

CUTTING

COTTON PRINT:
Cut 2 pieces 8″ × 14″ for base.

Cut 2 pieces 11″ × 14″ for the lining.

Cut 4 strips 3″ × 17″ for ties.

COORDINATING COTTON PRINT:
Cut 10 strips 1¼″ × width of fabric; seam together with a diagonal seam to make 1 long strip.

LIGHTWEIGHT FUSIBLE INTERFACING: Cut 4 strips 2″ × 17″ for ties.

HEAVYWEIGHT FUSIBLE FLEECE INTERFACING:
Cut 2 pieces 7″ × 13″.

Cut 2 pieces 10″ × 13″.

Construction

Prepare Boxed Corners

Cut a 2˝ square from the bottom corners of the base and lining pieces and of the heavyweight fusible fleece interfacing pieces.

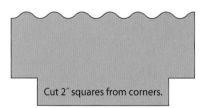

Cut 2˝ squares from corners.

Apply Interfacings

1. Place the lightweight fusible interfacing in the center of the wrong side of the ties. Fuse per manufacturer's instructions.

2. Center the heavyweight fusible fleece on the wrong side of the base and lining pieces. Fuse per manufacturer's instructions.

Make the Bag

Seam allowances are ⅜˝ unless otherwise noted.

MAKE THE BASE

1. With right sides facing, pin the base panels together. Sew the sides and bottom seam, leaving the corners open. Press seams in opposite directions.

2. Pull the corners open and line up the side and bottom seams. Stitch across the corner to create a boxed corner.

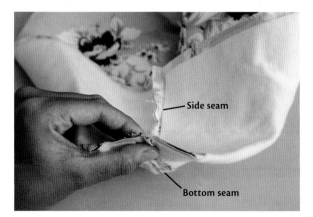

Side seam

Bottom seam

MAKE THE FABRIC ROPE
UPPER PORTION

Use a machine cording foot, if available.

1. Place one end of the laundry line or piping cord on the wrong side of one end of the coordinating cotton fabric strip. Fold about 1″ of the fabric over the cord that is centered inside the strip to create a finished edge.

2. With the cording in the center of the fabric strip, fold the fabric strip in half. Using a zipper foot, stitch about ⅛″ away from the cording to secure the cording in the fabric. If you don't have a zipper foot, adjust the needle position closer to the cord to achieve the same effect.

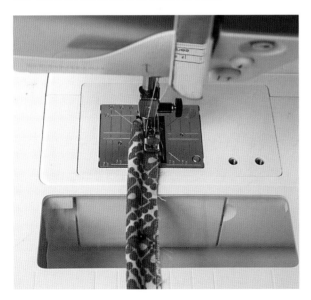

3. Beginning at a side seam, pin the raw edge of the cording fabric to the top of the bag base. Pin the strip most of the way around the bag.

4. Stitch the strip to the bag base using a straight stitch, snugging up the cording into the strip. Go around the bag, being careful to gently pull and keep the bag at its full size.

Tip

Use a zipper foot for the first row of cording or adjust the needle to the left or right to get as close as possible to the cording.

5. When you've reached the beginning of the cording, overlap the next row of cording next to or on top of the row you just sewed down. You will need to cross over the starting point and get the needle to the center where the 2 rows of rope meet.

6. If you used a zipper foot for the first row, change back to a universal foot now. Using a zigzag stitch, stitch down the center, catching both rows of cording. Continue to sew the cording around until you have 14 rows of cording.

Tip

Gently pull and stretch the bag as you go, to keep its full shape. Tilt and adjust the project in the machine as necessary; otherwise the top will start to get smaller. Stop often and check your work.

7. At the end of the 14th row, when you are back at a side seam, cut the cording, fold the end of fabric over the cording, and neatly sew down.

Decorative Touches

If you like, decorate the basket with fabric flowers. It is easier to do so before the bag is put together. You can make circle flowers (see below), rolled roses (see my website in Resources, page 111), or add fabric flowers of your choice.

CIRCLE FLOWERS

1. To make one circle flower, cut 2 circles 3″ in diameter (use a jar lid or similar item for a circle template).

2. With right sides facing, sew around the edges of the flower circles, leaving a 1″ opening for turning. Clip the curves. Turn the circles right side out and press.

3. Stitch a gathering stitch ¼″ from the edge around the circle and gently pull the thread to partially gather up the circle. Add a tiny bit of stuffing into the base of the flower and sew across the gathers to close up the flower, leaving the back of the flower ungathered and higher than the front.

4. Stitch the flowers to the bag and add felt leaves and twine as vine.

Put It Together

1. With right sides facing, pin the lining panels together. Sew the side seams and the bottom seam, leaving the corners open and a 6″ opening in the center of the bottom seam. Press the seams in opposite directions.

2. Pull the corners open and line up the side and bottom seams. Stitch across the corner to create a boxed corner.

3. To make the ties, fold the corners of one end to the center and press. Then fold over ½″ along each long edge and press. Then fold each tie in half lengthwise and press again. Stitch down the long edge and the point.

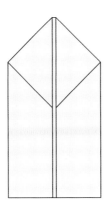

4. Determine which way you want to tie the basket to the bike; then place the ties in one of two ways:

- You can put ties on both the front and back, which will help keep the basket closed. Place the ties on the front and back 2″ from the side seams.

5. Place the lining and the bag right sides together, with the lining on the outside. Pin; then sew all around the top, close to the cording.

6. Pull the bag right side out through the opening in the lining. Stitch the opening closed.

7. Topstitch around the top of the bag in-the-ditch between the cording and the seam.

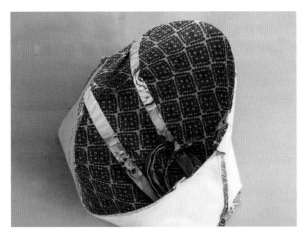

- You can tie it from the back only, leaving the front side open. Place pairs of ties on only the back, 2″ from side seams.

Out-of-Towner Tote

Finished tote: 22¼˝ wide × 15½˝ tall (not including purse strap) × 4¼˝ deep

I love how versatile this bag is for so many purposes. I began using a version of this bag as my "everyday purse"—no joke—when I was still in the stage of toting diapers, a change of clothes for all three kids, and snack stashes. It was just easier to have it all in one and hang this big old girl on my stroller handles. I adored my big bag.

It continues to be a great bag: perfect as a carry-on while traveling, excellent as an overnight bag to take to the grandparents' house, a great gift for the new graduate to take to college. The preteen will love it for a slumber party bag. It's just a fabulous all-purpose bag with loads of style. You will love keeping this for yourself or giving it away as a gift.

It features a zip pocket on the back, an adorable ruffle-topped slip pocket on the front, lots of interior slip pockets, scalloped edges, sides that tie, and a magnetic snap.

MATERIALS

EXTERIOR: 1¾ yards

LINING: 1½ yards

HEAVYWEIGHT FUSIBLE FLEECE INTERFACING: 1½ yards, such as Pellon 971F

MAGNETIC SNAP: 1

SWIVEL CLASP HARDWARE PIECES: 4, with a 1˝–1¼˝ opening for strap

PURSE STRAPS: 1 pair, at least 20˝ long

RIBBON: 7˝ of ⅛˝ wide for zipper pull (*optional*)

CUTTING

EXTERIOR:
Cut 2 pieces 14˝ × 23˝ for front and back.

Cut 1 piece 5˝ × 49½˝ for gusset.

Cut 4 pieces 8˝ × 9˝ for front ruffle pocket and back zip pocket.

Cut 1 piece 2½˝ × 16˝ for ruffle.

Cut 1 piece 1½˝ × 9˝ for zipper strip.

Cut 4 pieces 5˝ × 17˝ for straps.

Cut 2 pieces 3˝ × 33˝ for scallop trim.

Cut 4 pieces 2˝ × 10˝ for side ties.

LINING:
Cut 2 pieces 14˝ × 23˝ for front and back.

Cut 1 piece 5˝ × 49½˝ for gusset.

Cut 2 pieces 3˝ × 33˝ for scallop trim.

Cut 2 pieces 7½˝ × 23˝ for pocket.

HEAVYWEIGHT FUSIBLE FLEECE INTERFACING:
Cut 4 pieces 13˝ × 22˝ for front, back, and lining.

Cut 2 pieces 4˝ × 48½˝ for gusset.

Cut 2 pieces 7½˝ × 8½˝ for exterior pockets.

Cut 4 pieces 2¾˝ × 13˝ for straps.

Cut 1 piece 7˝ × 22˝ for pocket.

Construction

Seam allowances are ⅜″
unless otherwise noted.

Apply Interfacing

Following the manufacturer's instructions, center and fuse interfacing to the wrong sides of the following:

- Front and back panels
- Gussets
- Exterior pockets
- Lining pocket
- Straps (centered between long edges and ½″ from bottom edge)

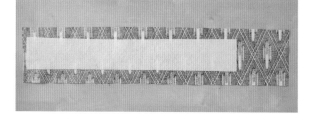

Make the Straps

1. Press strap over edges of interfacing. Then fold in half and press.

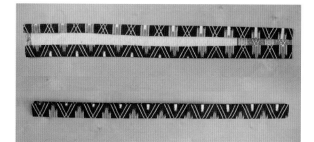

2. Slide the swivel clasp hardware onto the strap and fold the strap over where the interfacing ends. Pin and set strap aside.

Ruffle Pocket

1. With wrong sides facing, press the ruffle strip in half and gather it to the 8″ width of the pocket.

2. With raw edges matching, pin and then baste the ruffle in place.

3. With right sides facing, place the pocket lining on the pocket exterior with the ruffle in the middle. Pin and then stitch along the top edge.

4. Flip the pocket right side out, press, and topstitch ¼″ below the ruffle, along the edge of the pocket.

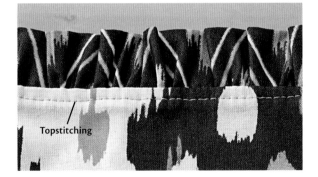

Topstitching

5. Center the ruffle pocket on the front panel, with the lower edge matching the front panel lower edge, and baste it in place.

Attach the Straps

1. Place each strap so it overlaps the pocket sides ½″ and covers the ends of the ruffle as well. The hardware on the strap

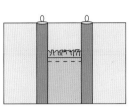

should be about ¼″ below the top edge of the main bag panel. Measure 1½″ down from the hardware and pin the strap to the bag at this mark. Measure 1½″ below this mark. Place another pin at that point—between these 2 pins, you will stitch a crisscrossed box to secure the strap. Remove any other pins.

2. Start stitching from the bottom of the bag up the strap ⅛″ from the edge. Stitch all the way up to the top pin. Pivot and stitch across the strap; then turn and continue down the opposite side to lower pin. Stop. Pivot and sew across the strap again, making a box. Turn sharply and stitch diagonally across the box to the upper corner, then across the top of the box again. Pivot and stitch diagonally across the box to the other corner and continue down the opposite side of strap to the bottom of bag. Stitch a second line of stitching ⅛″ from the first line, up the side of the strap, across the top of the box, and down the other side of the strap.

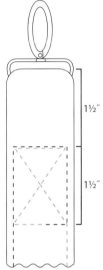

1½″

1½″

Follow stitching path from red to blue to green for first line of stitching.

3. Fold the bag out of the way and follow the stitch lines on the strap up to ½″ below the hardware, pivot, and stitch across and back down the opposite side. Stitch again, following the inner line of stitching and reinforcing the stitched line under the hardware. Repeat for the strap on the other side of the pocket. (For a video tutorial of this strap assembly step, see Resources, page 111.)

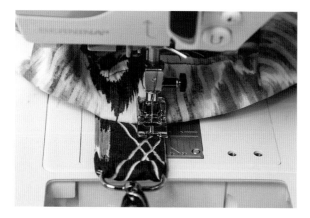

Back Exterior Zipper Pocket

1. Fold the long edges of the zipper strip to the center, press, and set it aside.

2. Make a zipper sandwich: Place the interfaced pocket panel right side up. Place the zipper with the right side facing that panel. Place the pocket lining panel right side facing the pocket fabric. Using a zipper foot, stitch the zipper. **Note:** *If you do not have a zipper foot, adjust the needle position to the left or right to make this step easier.*

3. Flip the pocket right side out, press, and topstitch ⅛″ from edge of seam.

4. Center the zipper pocket on the rear panel, with lower edges matching, and baste it in place.

5. Place the zipper strip on top of the zipper tape. Open the zipper a bit to move the zipper pull out of the way for stitching. Stitch along the top and bottom of the zipper strip to secure.

6. See Attach the Straps (page 71) to add the straps to the pocket in the same manner as you did for the front ruffle pocket.

Scallop Trim

1. Place the scallop trim pattern (page 75) at one end of one exterior scallop trim piece and trace just the curves of 2 scallops. Do not draw a line down to the straight edge. Move the pattern and trace 2 more scallops. Continue until you have drawn 11 scallops, filling the full length of the strip. Repeat for the remaining exterior and 2 scallop trim lining pieces.

2. Carefully cut along the scallop lines on each piece.

When cutting the scallop edge, clip straight down to the center of the V between the scallops. Cut from the top edge back to this V so that you are making small cuts rather than trying to maneuver evenly through in one cutting motion.

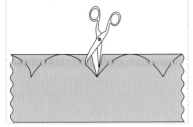

3. Place an exterior scallop trim piece and a lining scallop piece right sides facing and begin sewing at one corner, continuing along the 3″ edge and to the first scallop. Continue sewing each scallop and then down to the end corner. Do not sew the long straight edge. Repeat for the second pair of trim pieces.

Tip

To make it easier to stitch the scallops, mark a straight line at each V so you know where to pivot.

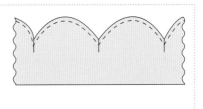

4. Clip into the V's as far down as you can without clipping the stitching. Clip the curves and turn the scallop trim piece right side out. Press; then topstitch ¼″ from the edge.

5. Gather the scallop trim and pin it to the exterior panels, right sides facing, stopping ½″ in from the edge. Baste the scallop trim in place with the edge of the last scallop just outside the side seam.

Put It Together

1. Make the side ties by pressing along the long edges to the center. Press the ends to form a triangle and press the ties in half. Stitch along the long edges and points.

2. Pin the ties 2″ below the top of the bag with raw edges matching and the ties to the inside of the bag.

Pin tie here.

3. Pin back the scallops to keep the edges from getting caught in the seam.

4. With right sides facing, pin the gusset to the exterior panel.

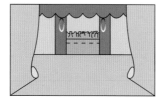

5. Stitch the gusset seam. Repeat for the rear panel and include the other set of ties.

6. To make the lining pocket, with right sides facing, create a tube by stitching along the long edges of the lining pocket. Turn the pocket right side out and press. Topstitch ½″ from the top of the pocket.

7. Measure 4″ from top of lining panel and pin the pocket in place. Divide the pockets as desired; for example, for 3 pockets, mark the pocket at about 7½″ from the end and again at 7½″ from that marking. Stitch along those marks to create a divided pocket. Reinforce the stitching at the pocket top at the stress points and sew along the pocket bottom.

8. Insert the gusset into the lining in the same manner as you did for the exterior of the bag in Steps 4 and 5, but leave a 9″ opening in the bottom seam of the gusset on one side for turning the bag.

9. To insert the magnetic snap into the lining, find the center of the lining along the top. Measure down 2″ from the center mark and insert half of the snap, following the manufacturer's instructions. Repeat for the other side, inserting the other half of the snap. Leave the lining wrong side out.

10. Pin the straps down on the exterior bag panel with the hardware pulled out of the way of the top seam. With the right sides facing, place the exterior of the bag inside the lining. Match the side seams and pin along the top edge, being careful not to catch the ruffled scallop edges in the seam. Stitch all around the top edge.

11. Pull the bag right side out through the opening in the lining. I like to say this is the point at which the bag is giving birth, because it's about to get really awesome at this stage.

12. Check the seams to be sure you have caught everything along the side seams, along the gussets, and all along the top. This is your chance to fix anything that went awry.

13. Stitch the opening in the lining closed. Push the lining into the bag. Press the top edge.

14. Topstitch around the top of the bag. Clip on the handles. Add a piece of ribbon to the zipper on the outer pocket or a cute pendant for a zipper pull.

Book a plane to someplace sunny, pack your bag, and get out of town!

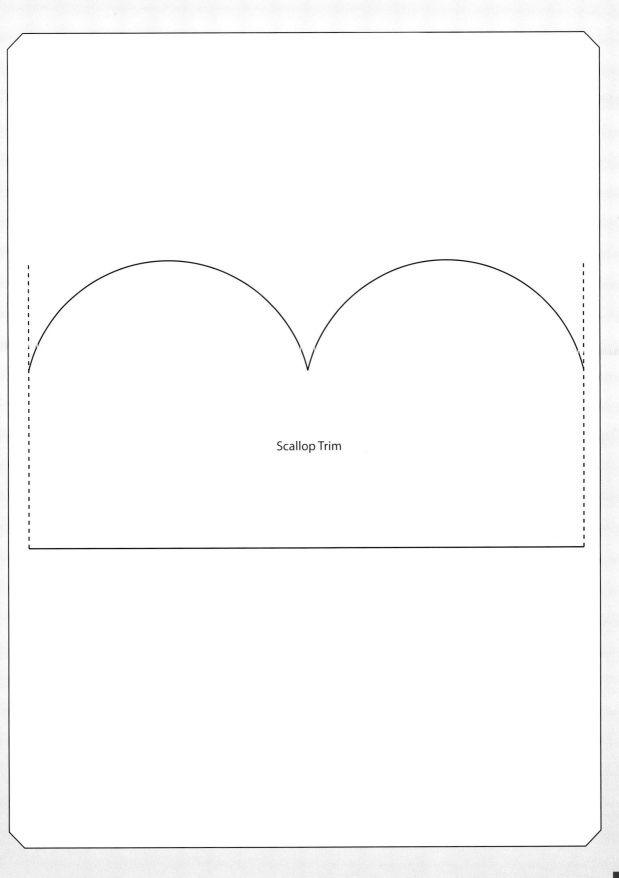

Scallop Trim

Sweet Tweet Bag

(A Birder's Best Friend)

Finished bag: 14½″ × 10¾″

Spring migration is a favorite time of year for me—I grew to love it from my time as a state park naturalist when I was in college. Lots of colorful birds are always dropping into the trees to rest on their long journey and sing sweet songs in the air. This little bag was inspired by that love of nature and hiking through the woods, watching for warblers. Featuring a little zip pocket on the front to hold your birder's life list and a slip pocket inside for your binoculars, this little bag will be a wonderful companion while out on the trail.

If you'd rather, omit the appliqué and glam it up for a daytime version for running around town on the concrete trails of the big city. Either way, this bag is sure to make the birds sing a sweet song, whether you are checking off your birder's life list or your grocery list.

MATERIALS

LINEN SOLID: ⅜ yard for front exterior

COTTON PRINT: ½ yard for front and back exterior

CONTRASTING COTTON PRINT 1: ¾ yard for lining

CONTRASTING COTTON PRINT 2: ½ yard for strap and optional back exterior

CONTRASTING COTTON PRINT 3: ½ yard for strap accent and optional back exterior

APPLIQUÉ FABRIC: scraps

LIGHTWEIGHT FUSIBLE INTERFACING: 1 package (20″ × 45″), such as Shape-Flex

HEAVYWEIGHT FUSIBLE FLEECE INTERFACING: ¾ yard, such as Pellon 971F

PAPER-BACKED FUSIBLE WEB

ZIPPER: 7″

MAGNETIC SNAP: 1

CUTTING

LINEN SOLID: Cut 1 using pattern piece A (pullout page P2).

COTTON PRINT:
Cut 1 using pattern piece B (pullout page P2).

Cut 1 piece for back after piecing front panel (Option 1).

CONTRASTING COTTON PRINT 1:
Cut 2 pieces 7½″ × 10″ for lining pocket.

Cut 2 pieces 8″ × 8″ for exterior zipper pocket.

Cut 2 pieces for lining after piecing front panel.

CUTTING continued on page 78

Construction

Seam allowances are ⅜″ unless otherwise noted.

Make the Panels

1. Fuse the lightweight interfacing to the wrong side of the lining pocket and exterior pocket.

2. With right sides facing, sew together pieces A and B to make the front panel. Press the seam open.

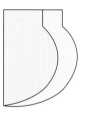

3. Use this pieced front panel as the pattern to cut a back exterior panel from either the main cotton fabric or contrasting cotton fabrics 2 or 3—your choice. Also cut 2 lining panels from contrasting cotton fabric 1. Then cut 4 pieces of fusible fleece ½″ smaller all the way around than the pieced front panel.

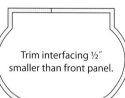

Trim interfacing ½″ smaller than front panel.

4. Fuse the fleece to wrong sides of the back exterior panel and both lining panels, following the manufacturer's instructions.

CUTTING (continued)

CONTRASTING COTTON PRINT 2:
Cut 1 strip 2⅜″ × 42″ (or desired length) for strap.

Cut 1 piece for back after piecing front panel (Option 2).

CONTRASTING COTTON PRINT 3:
Cut 1 strip 3¼″ × 42″ (or desired length) for strap accent.

Cut 1 piece for back after piecing front panel (Option 3).

LIGHTWEIGHT INTERFACING:
Cut 2 pieces 7″ × 10″ for lining pocket.

Cut 2 pieces 7½″ × 8″ for exterior pocket.

FUSIBLE FLEECE:
Cut 1 strip 2″ × 42″ (or desired length) for strap.

Cut 4 pieces after piecing front panel (see Step 2, at left).

Insert the Zipper and Pocket

1. Place the fleece, fusible side down, on the back of the pieced front and pin. Using a ruler, draw a line on the fleece, following the seam.

2. Draw a rectangle, using the line as the center, ½″ wide and 6½″ long. The rectangle should be placed 2″ from top and bottom of panel, centered on the seam. Remove the fleece from the front panel and cut along the rectangle lines, leaving a ½″ × 6½″ hole. Reposition the fleece on the back of the front panel, centering the hole over the seam, and fuse it in place.

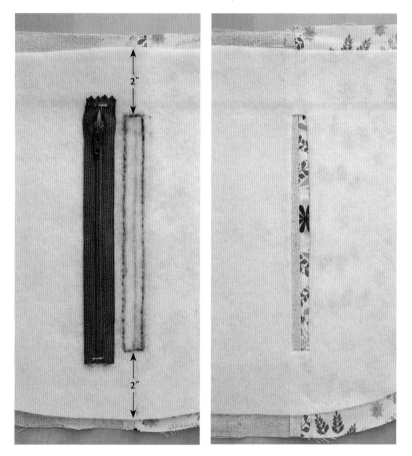

3. Stitch across the ends of the zipper, especially if you have cut down a longer zipper to 7″, so you don't lose the zipper off the end.

4. On the interfaced side of one exterior pocket piece, draw a rectangle 6½″ long and ½″ wide that is ½″ from a 7½″ edge and ½″ from the top and bottom. Draw triangles at both ends that come into the rectangle ¼″. Place this pocket wrong side up on the right side of the front exterior panel, over the seam and matching this rectangle to the one cut in the fleece. Be sure the center of the rectangle follows the seamline where you pieced together the panel.

5. Sew along the lines of the rectangle outline; do not sew on the center or triangle lines.

6. Carefully cut along the center line of the pocket, stopping at the triangles. Open the center seam of the bag with a seam ripper to ¼″ away from each end. Clip the corners, being careful not to cut the stitching.

7. Pull the pocket through the hole and press the seams to the inside of the bag.

8. Pin the zipper in place behind the hole, right side facing out, and topstitch ⅛″ from the edges.

9. Pin the second exterior pocket panel to the zippered one around all 4 sides. Stitch all 4 sides of the pocket, using ¼″ seams, without stitching it to the bag.

Add the Appliqué

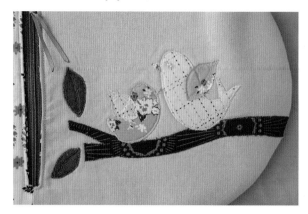

See the appliqué patterns (pullout page P2) for this project. Refer to A Few Words about Appliqué (page 110) to determine how to cut out and prepare the appliqué pieces.

Prepare the appliqué using the method of your choice. Be sure to move the pocket out of the way so as not to catch it in your stitching. I used corduroy for the leaves and beads for eyes to add texture and interest. Be creative in the fabric textures you use to create depth to your image.

Make the Lining

1. With right sides facing, pin the lining pocket panels together. Sew around all 4 sides, leaving a 4″ opening in the bottom for turning. Clip the corners. Turn the pocket right side out and press, being sure to turn in the opening in the bottom. Topstitch across the top of the pocket with 2 rows of stitching.

2. Center the pocket on one of the lining panels. Pin and stitch it in place, backstitching at stress points to secure.

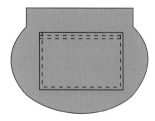

3. With right sides facing, pin together the lining panels. Stitch, leaving the top open and leaving a 6″ opening in the bottom for turning. Clip the curves and inside corners.

4. Leave the lining wrong side out. Find the center along one top edge of the lining. Measure 2″ down from the center and mark. Following the manufacturer's instructions, place half of the magnetic snap at this point. Repeat for the opposite lining panel, matching the first snap half.

Make the Strap

1. With right sides facing, pin together the 2 strap strips along one long edge. Stitch. Match up long edges on the opposite side of the strap and pin as shown. Stitch.

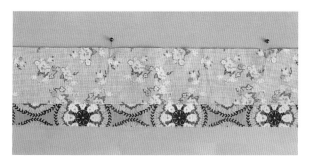

2. Turn the strap right side out and press so the narrow strip is edged with fabric from the other side.

3. Using a safety pin, thread the fleece into the strap. Following the manufacturer's instructions, press to fuse the interfacing inside the strap.

4. Topstitch the edges of the strap.

Put It Together

1. With right sides facing, pin together the exterior panels. Stitch along the sides, leaving the top open. Clip the curves and inside corners, turn right side out, and press.

2. With right sides facing, pin the strap to the exterior of the bag, centering the strap to the side seam and raw edges even. Be sure the strap is not twisted as you sew each side.

Tip

After you have sewn the strap on, pin the strap, pulled straight down along the seam, about 2″ below the top. This will hold the strap evenly in place while you sew the bag together.

3. With the exterior right side out and the lining wrong side out, place the exterior *inside* the lining so that right sides are facing. Pin and then stitch all the way around the top. Make sure the strap is pulled down and out of the way of this seam.

4. Pull the bag through the opening in the lining until the bag is completely right side out. Sew the opening in the lining closed. Push the lining into the bag. Press and topstitch along the top edge of the bag.

Junior Ranger Backpack

Finished backpack: 9¼″ wide × 14⅞″ tall × 3″ deep

Would it surprise you to know that before my sewing career, I was a park ranger? Oh yes, as in the cool hat, the badge, the car with the red and blue lights—the whole thing. My first job out of college landed me at Glacier National Park in Montana. Coolest. Job. Ever.

I married a park ranger. And together we are raising our own crew of junior rangers. We live on five acres that include a creek, woodlands, a pasture, and plenty of open space for our kids to explore all the wonders that nature provides us with each passing season (I try not to squeal when they bring baby snakes or toads to the back porch).

Of course, every junior ranger needs his or her own backpack for these backyard and wilderness adventures. This backpack is also an awesome mom bag because it keeps your hands free so you can round up all your junior rangers. I love using mine in the summer when we are shopping in town at the farmers' market or walking through the summer fairs. These bags are a quick project and make great gifts for a summer camper, day hiker, or farmers' market explorer. They are so easy that you can even make several for favors at a birthday party!

MATERIALS

COTTON PRINT 1: ½ yard for exterior

COTTON PRINT 2: ½ yard for lining, strap casings, and loops

COTTON PRINT 3: ½ yard for straps

HEAVYWEIGHT FUSIBLE FLEECE INTERFACING: ½ yard, such as Pellon 971F, for exterior panel

LIGHTWEIGHT FUSIBLE INTERFACING: 1 package (20″ × 45″), such as Shape-Flex

CUTTING

COTTON PRINT 1: Cut 2 pieces 13″ × 15½″.

COTTON PRINT 2:
Cut 2 pieces 13″ × 15½″ for lining.

Cut 2 strips 4″ × 12½″ for strap casings.

Cut 2 pieces 2½″ × 2½″ for bottom strap loops.

COTTON PRINT 3: Cut 4 strips 3″ × width of fabric.

HEAVYWEIGHT FUSIBLE FLEECE INTERFACING: Cut 2 pieces 12″ × 14½″.

LIGHTWEIGHT FUSIBLE INTERFACING:
Cut 2 pieces 12″ × 14½″.

Cut 2 pieces 2½″ × 2½″.

Construction

Seam allowances are ⅜″ unless otherwise noted.

1. Cut out a 1½″ × 1½″ square from the bottom corners of the exterior and lining panels, and the interfacing and fleece pieces.

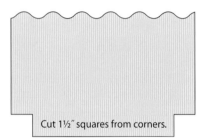

Cut 1½″ squares from corners.

2. Center the fusible fleece on the wrong side of the exterior panels. Fuse, following the manufacturer's instructions. Repeat with the lightweight fusible interfacing on the wrong side of the lining panels.

3. Make the strap casings: Press under the short ends ½″ and topstitch ⅛″ from the fold. With the wrong sides facing, fold the casings in half along the long edges.

4. Center each casing on an exterior panel along the top. Pin and then baste the casings using a ⅛″ seam allowance.

5. Make the bottom strap loops: Fuse the 2½″ lightweight fusible interfacing squares to the wrong side of the 2½″ fabric squares. Press under ½″ on 2 opposite sides. Topstitch ⅛″ along the pressed edges; then fold in half crosswise.

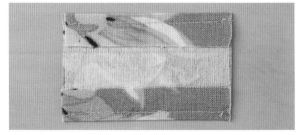

6. Pin the strap loops 1˝ up from the cutout in the bottom corners on each side of one exterior panel and baste them in place.

7. With right sides facing, pin together the exterior panels. Sew along the sides and the bottom.

8. Fold together the openings in the bottom corners of the bag, matching the side and bottom seams, and pin. Sew to close the corners, creating a boxed bottom. Turn the backpack right side out.

9. With right sides facing, pin together the lining panels. Sew the sides, the bottom, and the corners as you did the exterior, except leave a 6˝ opening in the bottom for turning the backpack.

10. Put the exterior of the bag *inside* the lining of the bag, with right sides facing, matching the side seams and top of the bag. Be sure to keep strap casings flat on the bag and out of the seamline. Pin.

11. Sew all the way around the top edge.

12. Pull the bag right side out through the opening in the lining. Check all the seams along the top and sides. Correct any mistakes before sewing the lining opening closed.

13. Press the top seam and topstitch ⅛˝ away from the seam on the bag (not the casing), all the way around the bag, and then stitch a second row ⅛˝ away from the first.

14. Sew the opening in the lining closed.

15. With right sides together, sew together 2 pairs of the strap pieces to create 2 long pieces. Press under the long edges of each strap piece ½˝.

16. Fold in the corners at the ends of the strap pieces and press. Fold each strip in half lengthwise and topstitch along the long edges and the point ends.

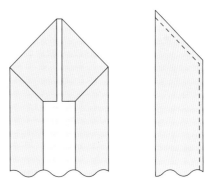

17. Insert a strap through one casing and back through the second casing, with ends open to the right. Insert the other strap with ends open to the left. Insert the ends of each strap through the bottom strap loops. Pull both straps to fully close the bag and then adjust the length as desired by tying a knot or bow in the end of straps below the loop.

Father Knows Best Bag

Finished bag: 5¾˝ wide × 10½˝ long × 5˝ tall

It can be a challenge to find appropriate sewing projects for the guys in your life. Guys aren't so much into patchwork and cute frilly things. But I think this boxed bag is a perfect idea. Both my dad and husband use one to put all their "man stuff" in when they travel.

One of the added details is to use an old key for the zipper pull. It represents the key to your heart that this special guy holds. I like the idea of using a heavy canvas fabric for this project to make it sturdier. Guys can be a bit rough. Add a special touch to this bag by printing a special quote or message on printable fabric sheets and stitching it inside the lining of the bag. You might consider using a laminated fabric or oilcloth for the interior as well.

MATERIALS

COTTON OR CANVAS: ½ yard for exterior and strap

CONTRASTING COTTON OR CANVAS: ½ yard for lining

HEAVYWEIGHT FUSIBLE FLEECE INTERFACING: ½ yard, such as Pellon 971F

ZIPPER: 16˝ (polyester)

OLD KEY OR DECORATIVE ZIPPER PULL

CUTTING

COTTON OR CANVAS:
Cut 1 piece 16˝ × 21˝ for exterior.

Cut 1 piece 6½˝ × 6½˝ for strap.

CONTRASTING COTTON OR CANVAS:
Cut 1 piece 16˝ × 21˝ for lining.

Cut 1 piece 2˝ × 2˝ for pull tab.

FUSIBLE FLEECE INTERFACING:
Cut 2 pieces 15˝ × 20˝.

Construction

Seam allowances are ⅜″ unless otherwise noted.

Tip

Sew across the ends of your zipper, if necessary, to prevent the zipper from coming undone and off the track.

1. Press the strap in half with wrong sides facing. Open and then press the edges to the center crease. Press in half again and pin. Topstitch ⅛″ from the folded edges.

2. Center the interfacing pieces on the wrong sides of the main panel and lining. Fuse, following the manufacturer's instructions.

3. Make a zipper sandwich: Place the exterior fabric right side up. Place the zipper facedown along the 16″ edge with the top of the zipper to the right. Place the lining right side facing the exterior. Pin the layers in place. Stitch along the top edge, starting ½″ from the end and stopping ½″ from the other end.

Note: *If you have a zipper foot, use it for this step. If you do not have a zipper foot, adjust the needle position to the left or right to make this step easier.*

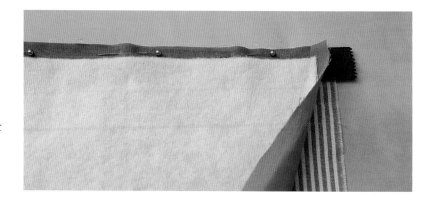

4. Turn the bag right side out. Press and topstitch along the edge of the zipper.

5. Fold the raw edge of the exterior panel up, opposite the zipper and with right sides facing, and pin to the other side of the zipper. Repeat for the lining, creating 2 tubes. Pin and sew the panels to the zipper, again starting your stitching ½˝ from one end and stopping ½˝ from the other end.

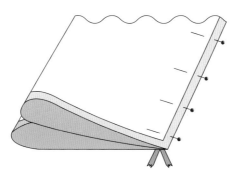

Tip

When stitching through heavy multiple layers, use a stitch length of 3.0–3.5. This will allow your needle to get through all the layers and back up before advancing to the next stitch. A jeans or denim needle is handy to use on projects with thick layers.

6. Open the zipper and turn the bag right side out, press along the zipper edge, and topstitch.

7. Turn the entire bag wrong side out. With the zipper in the center, your bag will resemble a tube on top and bottom (exterior and lining). Fold both flat; then pin the edges keeping the exterior and lining separate.

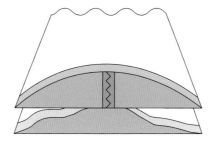

8. Create the pull tab by pressing the 2″ × 2″ square in half, wrong sides facing. Open and then press 2 edges to the center crease. Press in half again.

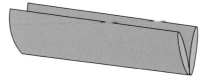

9. Topstitch ⅛″ from each folded edge. Fold the piece in half crosswise to create the pull tab and baste it along the raw edge.

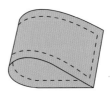

10. Center the pull tab over the end of the zipper in the exterior layer, matching the raw edges. Pin the tab in place. Turn over and fold the lining back and pin it out of the way. Sew the exterior closed along the edge with the pull tab, underneath the zipper and between the exterior layers.

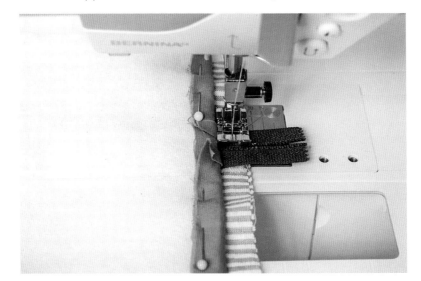

11. Pull the exterior back and pin it out of the way. Sew the lining closed on this end.

On the other end, pull the exterior back out of way and pin it back. Sew the lining closed.

12. Move the lining back and pin it out of the way. Sew the exterior closed on this last opening.

13. Flatten the bag and cut out 2″ × 2″ squares on each corner.

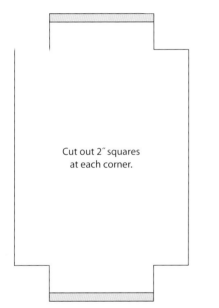

Cut out 2″ squares at each corner.

14. Thread the strap into the bag through the corner opening on the exterior. Center the strap over the seam. Pin. Fold together the corners of only the exterior and sew the seam (sewing the strap in place at same time) to create a boxed corner. Repeat on the opposite corner of the exterior, sewing in the other end of the strap.

Then sew one corner of the lining, leaving the last corner in the lining open.

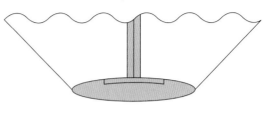

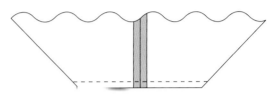

15. Stitch over all the layers on each end at the zipper, if necessary, to secure any openings.

16. Pull the bag through the opening in the lining. Turn the bag right side out. Push out the corners, reaching inside the bag through the opening as necessary. Hand or machine stitch the last corner of the lining opening closed.

17. Push the lining inside the bag.

18. Add the decorative pull to the zipper.

Hotty Totty Casserole Carrier

Finished carrier: fits a 9″ × 13″ dish

Well, you Hotty Totty, you! It's kind of a naughty name for a fun casserole carrier, don't you think? Whether for the school party, a neighborhood picnic, a potluck at work, or a gathering of friends at the lake, this little carrier is both functional and great looking.

I imagine this as a great gift for a friend who is newly married or new to your neighborhood. Or maybe for a friend who is recuperating from an illness— How fabulous would it be to show up with dinner in a cute carrier that they can keep and use again?

It's easy to adjust this pattern for various sizes of pans you might have on hand and make a matching set.

(Psst! If you love the look of this casserole carrier, check out my free tutorial for the Summer Sunday Bag—the purse that inspired this project; see Resources, page 111.)

MATERIALS

COTTON PRINT 1 (FLORAL): 1⅜ yards for main exterior

COTTON PRINT 2 (RED STRIPE): 1⅜ yards for exterior patchwork and lining

COTTON PRINT 3 (ORANGE CHEVRON): ¼ yard for exterior patchwork

HOOK-AND-LOOP TAPE: 5½″ length

METALIZED MYLAR INSULATED INTERFACING: 1 package or ¾ yard, such as Insul-Fleece (by C&T Publishing)

HARD PURSE HANDLES: a minimum of 8½″ wide (I used bamboo handles 8½″ × 5½″.)

CUTTING

COTTON PRINT 1:
Cut 1 piece 7½″ × 36½″ for exterior panel.

Cut 1 piece 11″ × 43¾″ for interior panel.

COTTON PRINT 2:
Cut 1 piece 3″ × 36½″ for exterior panel.

Cut 1 piece 11″ × 43¾″ for lining.

Cut 1 piece 13½″ × 36½″ for lining.

COTTON PRINT 3:
Cut 1 piece 4½″ × 36½″ for exterior panel.

INSULATED INTERFACING:
Cut 1 piece 11″ × 43¾″ for interior panel.

Cut 1 piece 13½″ × 30½″ for exterior panel.

Construction

Seam allowances are ⅜″ unless otherwise noted.

Preparation

1. Sew together the 36½″-long pieces of fabrics 1, 2, and 3 to form 1 piece 13½″ × 36½″ for the outside of the exterior panel. Press the seams to one side.

2. Round all the corners of the exterior, interior, linings, and interior insulated interfacing pieces using the corner pattern (page 97) or a 6″ saucer as a guide.

Make the Interior Panel

1. Place the interior piece right side up with the lining on top right side down. Add the insulated fleece interfacing with shiny side facing down. Pin together the layers.

Tip

Sew with the insulated interfacing side up and the fabric side down on the sewing machine. The interfacing tends to stick on the sewing machine plate, and that could pull and pucker your fabric. Sewing with the fleece side up helps the feed dogs to work better.

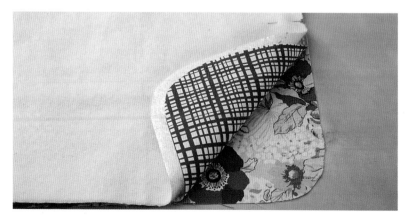

2. Sew all the way around, leaving a 7″ opening in the center of one long side for turning. Clip the curves.

3. Turn the interior panel right side out. Press and topstitch all the way around, closing the opening on the edge.

4. On the lining side, place a 1½″ piece of hook-and-loop tape on one end, centered and ½″ from the edge. Place a 4″ piece of hook-and-loop tape centered and 8″ below the bottom edge of this piece. Stitch down the hook-and-loop tape pieces.

5. Turn this panel lining side down and, on the opposite end, place a 4″ piece of hook-and-loop tape centered and ½″ from the edge. Place a 1½″ piece of hook-and-loop tape 8″ below the lower edge of this piece. Pin the tape in place and fold over the panel to check that the pieces match up. It is helpful to place a 9″ × 13″ pan on your panel to make sure that your tape closures will work and match up. Adjust as necessary. Stitch the tape in place.

Make the Exterior Panel

1. Place the exterior piece right side up with the lining on top right side down. Add the insulated fleece interfacing with shiny side facing down, centering it between the short edges. There will be 3″ of fabric extending beyond the interfacing on each end. Pin together the layers.

2. Sew all the way around, leaving a 7″ opening in the center of one long side for turning. Clip the curves.

3. Turn the carrier right side out. Press and topstitch all the way around.

4. To hold the interfacing in place, stitch through all layers 3″ from each end. You can mark this line with an erasable marker if necessary.

Add the Handle

1. Fold the 3″ of fabric that extends beyond the interfacing over the handle at the stitching line of the interfacing and toward the right side of the panel. Pin.

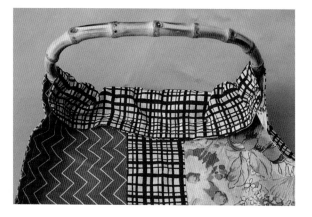

2. Sew close to the handle. Stitch slowly, continuously smoothing the fabric as you sew and moving the handle as needed.

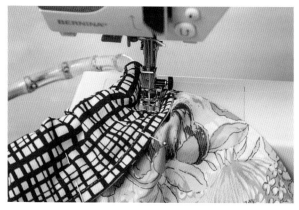

3. Repeat on the other side for the other handle.

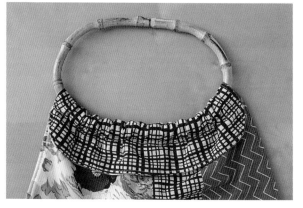

Tip

Pin and then move the handle around, smoothing the fabric as you put in the next pin. It takes some wiggling to find the best angle to get the fabric pinned.

Put It Together

1. Fold the exterior panel in half crosswise (handle to handle) and mark the center along each side with a pin. Unfold and lay flat with lining side up.

2. Fold the interior panel lengthwise, lining side in the center. Place this fold along the center of the exterior panel you just marked with the pins. Slide the interior panel so that the end with the hook-and-loop tape on the lining side is 13″ from the edge of the exterior panel. Unfold and pin together the panels.

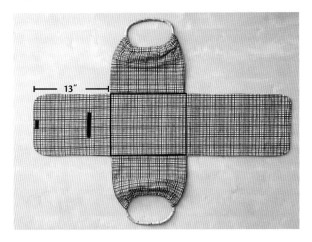

Tip

Stitch the panels together along the top edges you can see—2 short edges from the outside and 2 long edges from the lining side. Then you can stitch a second box inside these, following your first stitching lines as a guide.

Load up your mother's secret recipe for mac-n-cheese and off to the party!

3. Stitch the panels together where they cross in a box shape with double lines of stitching to secure the 2 panels in place.

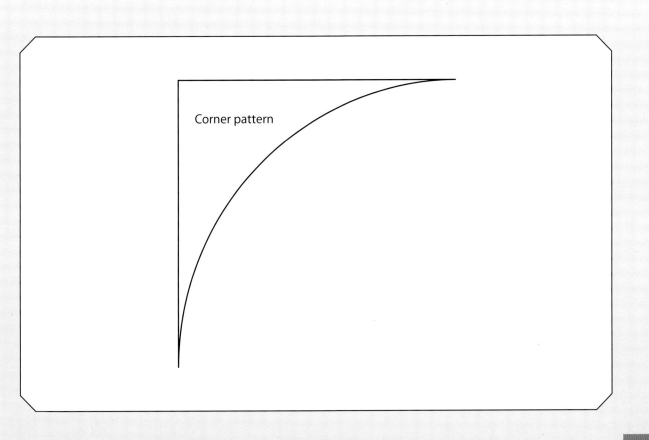

Corner pattern

Vintage Ice Skate Christmas Stocking

Finished stocking: 18″ × 20″ (ice skate),
11″ × 17″ (cowboy boot)

When my husband and I had a life BK (you know, Before Kids), one of our favorite date-night activities was ice-skating. I was a pathetically horrible hockey player in college but great skater, as was my husband. We would chase each other around the rink as fast as we could and then hold hands when the lights were turned down low during a slow song. Good memories. Those date nights on skates inspired this Christmas stocking. Hang it on your wall for some sweet winter decor or hang it by your fireplace for old St. Nick to fill.

Fabric note: A nice, solid flannel or textured fabric works well for the wintry feel of this project. The flannel is lovely to quilt on.

MATERIALS

FLANNEL OR TEXTURED FABRIC: ½ yard for exterior boot

COTTON: ¼ yard for inner sock

FLANNEL OR COTTON: ¼ yard for skate blade (omit for cowboy boot)

FELT: ⅛″ yard or 9″ × 12″ piece for boot sole

RIBBON: 16½″ length for cuff (omit for cowboy boot)

HEAVYWEIGHT FUSIBLE FLEECE INTERFACING: ½ yard, such as Pellon 971F

PRINT OR SOLID COTTONS: 2 different fat quarters for cuff and boot appliqués (omit for cowboy boot)

PAPER-BACKED FUSIBLE WEB

POLYESTER FIBERFILL: for stuffing

RIBBON: 6″ length for hanging tab

TRIM: velvet ribbon, buttons, lace, or other (*as desired*)

CUTTING

See the patterns (pullout page P3) for this project. Be careful when cutting the boot, boot sole, and blade; be sure to cut 2 that are facing opposite directions.

BOOT:
Cut 2 each of boot, boot sole, inner sock lining, and blade.

Cut 6 laces.

Cut 1 boot toe (*optionally, cut another of lace*).

Cut 1 boot heel (*optionally, cut another of lace*).

CUTTING continued on page 100

Vintage Ice Skate Christmas Stocking

Construction

Seam allowances are ⅜″ unless otherwise noted. Refer to A Few Words about Appliqué (page 110) to determine how to cut out and prepare the appliqué pieces.

1. Following the manufacturer's instructions, fuse interfacing to wrong side of boot pieces.

2. Appliqué the heel and toe fabrics in place on the front of the boot using the appliqué method of your choice. On the sample shown here, lace fabric was layered with a cotton fabric for the toe and heel appliqué.

3. Measure 5″ down from the top right edge of the boot and mark with a pin. This is where the 6 appliquéd laces will begin. Place the laces on the boot as shown and appliqué them in place.

CUTTING (continued)

CUFF:
Cut 2 rectangles 4½″ × 8¼″ for main cuff.

Cut 2 rectangles 2½″ × 8¼″ for cuff trim.

Cut 16″ piece of ribbon (*optional*).

HEAVYWEIGHT FUSIBLE FLEECE INTERFACING:
Cut 2 of boot.

4. Embellish the front of the boot as desired, adding quilting or decorative stitches as well as buttons and trims.

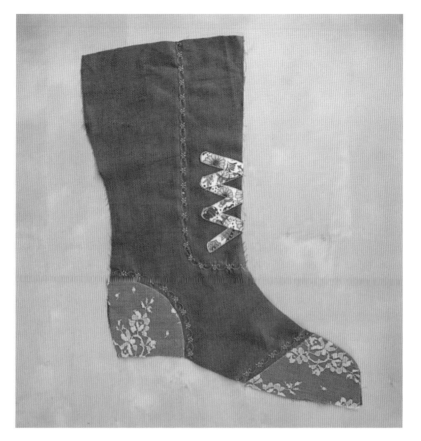

5. Carefully, using a lot of pins, pin the boot sole to the bottom of the boot. (I know it looks absolutely as if it will not fit, but trust me, it does.) Begin pinning at the heel and curve the fabric as needed to make the raw edges meet. Sew using a ¼˝ seam allowance; then clip the curves. Repeat for both the front and back of the boot.

6. With right sides facing, pin together the inner sock pieces. Sew the inner sock, leaving the top open. Set it aside.

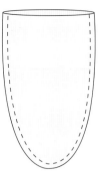

7. Make the cuff: With right sides facing, pin together one main cuff and one cuff trim piece along the long edge and stitch. Press seam open. Press under the lower edge of the cuff trim ¼″ and then fold this edge up to the seam. Topstitch ⅛″ from the seam to secure. Add ribbon embellishment as desired, making sure to sew it evenly on each side. Repeat for the second cuff piece.

8. With right sides facing, pin together the front and back cuff pieces along the short edges, matching the seams and trims. Sew, press seams to one side, and set aside.

9. With *wrong* sides facing, pin together the skate blade pieces. Using a small zigzag stitch ⅛″ from the edge, stitch together the blade, leaving the tops open where the blade joins the boot.

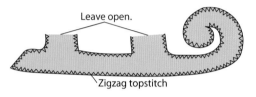

Leave open.

Zigzag topstitch

10. Stuff the blade gently with fiberfill until the blade is firm. Baste openings closed.

11. Pin the blade to the boot front, matching raw edges with the rear blade opening at heel of the boot and the front blade opening 2½″ from the toe end of the boot. Baste the blade in place. After basting, fold and pin the ends of the blade back onto the boot to keep it from getting caught in the seams in the next step.

12. With right sides facing, pin together the boot front and back, making sure the blade is tucked in and out of the way of the seams. Also, check that the boot sole is lined up and matching from front to back. Stitch along the boot sole using a ¼″ seam allowance. Using ¼″ seams, stitch the sides of the boot. Turn the boot right side out.

13. Tack the tip of the skate blade to the toe of the boot with hand stitching.

14. Fill the boot bottom with fiberfill up to the point where the inner sock will fall, just below the laces.

Putting It Together

1. For the Ice Skate, with *wrong* sides facing, insert the inner sock into the boot so that the raw edges match along the top and the side seams match. The right side of the sock will be visible when peering into the boot.

2. Fold the ribbon for the hanging tab in half and baste it to the top of the inner sock at the back seam, opposite the laces.

3. With right sides facing and side seams matching, layer the cuff inside the inner sock with the raw edges aligned.

Tip

Use fabric paint to add names on the stocking.

4. Pin together the layers and sew around the top edge.

5. Pull up the cuff and fold it over the boot.

6. For the cowboy boot, turn under ⅜″ around the top of the boot and the top of inner sock and press. Slip the inner sock inside the boot and pin the upper edges together, matching the seams. Fold the ribbon for the hanging tab in half and slip it between the boot and inner sock at the back seam, opposite the laces. Topstitch ⅛″ away from the pressed edges.

Joyful Hands Christmas Tree Skirt

Finished tree skirt: 45½″ diameter

When our family was brand new, with two little babies in the house, we started to think about what traditions we wanted to have for our own family. After the blur of taking care of newborn twins, I started to think clearly again somewhere around their second birthday. At Christmas that year, on a whim, we traced their handprints onto the skirt for our tree. I wrote the date and their names, and just like that, a new tradition was born. This last year, we added Grandma's hands. Everyone loves seeing how his or her hands have grown from one year to the next. To have those memories encircling our Christmas tree makes each year especially joyful.

MATERIALS

COTTON PRINTS AND/OR SOLIDS: ½ yard each of 4 or 8 fabrics* or 8 fat quarters

MUSLIN: 2¼ yards for ruffle and backing (at least 42″ wide)

BATTING: 1¼ yards, at least 42″ wide (I like Warm and Natural.)

RIBBON: 2½ yards of ⅝″ grosgrain, satin, or velvet for ties (or create your own using fabric)

PAPER-BACKED FUSIBLE WEB

* Due to the shape of the panel, you need ½ yard for either 1 or 2 panels.

CUTTING

COTTON PRINTS/SOLIDS: Cut 8 skirt panels using the pattern (pullout page P4).

½ yard will fit 2 panels

MUSLIN: Cut 6 strips 5″ × width of fabric.

NOTE: *Batting and backing pieces will be cut later using the assembled skirt front as a pattern.*

Because I Love You Sew

Construction

Seam allowances are ⅜″ unless otherwise noted.

Piece the Skirt and Cut the Backing and Batting

1. With right sides facing, piece together the skirt panels, leaving the last seam unsewn. Press the seams open.

2. Using the pieced skirt as a guide, cut 1 circle of the backing fabric, and 1 circle of the batting. Place the backing fabric right side up on top of the batting and set aside. Do *not* cut out the center circle or the open ends of the backing or batting; leaving these in place helps to stabilize the tree skirt while you sew the backing in place.

3. Place the center circle pattern (pullout page P4) in the center of the pieced skirt and pin it in place. Cut out the center.

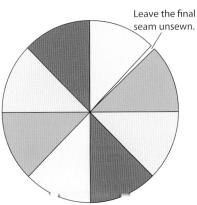

Leave the final seam unsewn.

Tip

Save the center circle. Stitch the final seam; then find your best little-girl friend and give her the center, which is now a perfect patchwork rug for a doll house or a special toy.

Embellish

See the tree appliqué patterns (pullout page P4) for this project. Refer to A Few Words about Appliqué (page 110) to determine how to cut out and prepare the appliqué pieces.

Appliqué and personalize as desired:

- Use the tree appliqué patterns provided or make your own designs.

- Trace your family members' hands.

- Write names and dates with stitching, hand embroidery, machine embroidery, or fabric paint.

To avoid having one huge
ruffle to work with, break
it into 4 smaller areas.
Before gathering the
ruffle, fold it in half and
mark this halfway point;
then fold in half again
and mark these quarter-
points on the ruffle with
pins. Match the ends of
the ruffle to the ends of
the skirt and the quarter
marks to the seamlines
of every 2 panels. Gather
and pin each section of
one-quarter the length of
the ruffle, breaking off
the gathering thread and
starting again each time.

Make and Add the Ruffle

1. Piece together the 6 strips to create a length of 7 yards.

2. Press under the short ends ¼" twice and sew to secure the hem.

3. Press the ruffle strip in half longwise so it is 2½" wide.

4. Gather the fabric evenly to fit the exterior edge of the skirt. If you have a ruffling foot for your machine, this is a good time to use it. Otherwise, follow these steps:

- Use a heavy thread, such as carpet thread, buttonhole thread, or thread used for denim.

- Tie a knot in the end of the gathering thread and place it on top of the ruffle ⅛" from the raw edge.

- Zigzag *over* the gathering thread, being careful not to sew *into* the thread. Pull on the heavy thread and gather the ruffled edge.

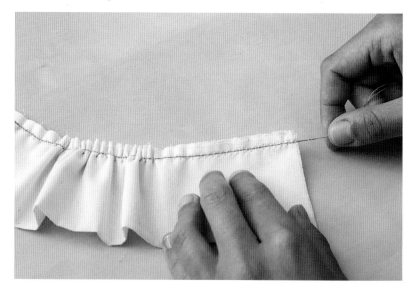

5. Pin the ruffle to the right side of the outer edge of the skirt, matching raw edges and placing the hemmed ends of the ruffle ⅜" from the end panel edges. Sew in place with a ¼" seam.

Put It Together

1. Cut the ribbon into 4 equal lengths, each 22½″ long. Matching raw edges, baste 2 pieces of ribbon along the open side of the skirt, placing them 3″ from the top and bottom. Baste the other 2 pieces of ribbon on the other open side. Pin back the ribbons to keep them out of the end panel seams for the next step.

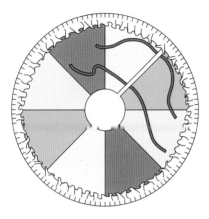

2. With right sides facing, place the skirt on top of the backing fabric and batting that were layered earlier. Pin through all layers around the outside circle, the end panels, and the inner circle, carefully keeping the ruffle out of the end panel seams.

3. Using a walking foot, if available, start sewing on an end panel at A and sew all around, stopping at B on the same end panel where you began, leaving a 7″ opening for turning.

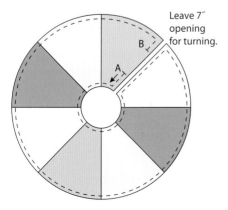

Leave 7″ opening for turning.

4. Trim the backing fabric and batting to the seam allowance at the end panels and cut out the center circle. Clip the edges all around both the center circle and outer circle, being careful not to cut into the stitch line, to allow the edge of the skirt to lie neatly when turned right side out.

5. Turn the skirt right side out. Press the seams and topstitch ¼″ on each side of each panel seam, and then ¼″ from the ruffled edge. You may also quilt around the appliqués as desired.

Gather around the Christmas tree and enjoy the holiday.

A Few Words about Appliqué

A number of the projects in this book are appliquéd. If you already have a favorite method for doing appliqué, go for it and use what you know. If you are new to appliqué, following are two easy applique methods that will work for any of the projects in this book.

Fusible Appliqué

Fusible appliqué using paper-backed fusible web is a quick and easy method.

1. Draw or trace the appliqué shape or design *in reverse* on the paper side of the paper-backed fusible web.

2. Cut out the shape with a ¼˝ margin around all the edges.

3. Following the manufacturer's instructions, iron the cut-out fusible to the *back* of the selected fabrics.

4. Cut out the shape on the drawn line.

5. Position the appliqué in place and iron (following the manufacturer's instructions) to fuse in place.

6. You can leave the edges of the appliqué raw or stitch over them with a straight stitch, a zigzag or satin stitch, or a blanket stitch.

Quick Turned-Edge Appliqué

If you prefer the turned-edge look, using Wash-Away Appliqué Sheets (by C&T Publishing) is an easy way to get this finished look. Be sure to follow the manufacturer's instructions.

1. Draw or copy the appliqué designs *in reverse* onto the dull, paper side of the Wash-Away Appliqué Sheets.

2. Cut out the shapes and iron them to the *back* of the selected fabrics.

3. Cut out the fabric with a ⅜˝ turn-under allowance.

4. Fold the turn-under allowance over the edge of the paper; finger-press or iron to hold the fold. If needed, use a dab of water-soluble or basting glue.

5. Pin the appliqués in place and stitch down by hand or machine.

Tip

To keep the fabric from buckling, you may want to use an embroidery stabilizer when stitching the appliqué to your item. Ask at your fabric or craft store for the appropriate type.

About the Author

Trish Preston is a sewing pattern designer and lover of old, rusty, interesting, colorful, and eclectic stuff that most people would just throw away. She holds a bachelor of science degree in environment and natural resources and put her studies to use as a park ranger and police officer for 12 years in national, state, and municipal parks, always crafting and sewing between shifts.

She launched her successful sewing pattern line in 2010 under the label Two Peas in a Pod Homegrown Designs, and she has appeared in several international magazines as well as on the television show *It's Sew Easy*. She married her handsome park ranger husband, and together they live on a pretty little piece of land in the country just outside of Columbus, Ohio, with their identical twin daughters, the Two Peas, and their youngest girl, whom they refer to as Sprout.

Visit Trish at twopeasinapoddesigns.com, where she journals about her life in the country, love of the earth, and all things related to sewing and crafting.

RESOURCES

The first place to go for information and products is your local quilt shop. If that is not possible or they cannot help you, then try the Internet.

TWO PEAS IN A POD HOMEGROWN DESIGNS
(Trish's website—printable labels, book tags, and recipe cards; bow-tie hardware; instructions for making rolled roses; video tutorials for tote strap assembly and Summer Sunday Bag—and so much more!)
twopeasinapoddesigns.com

AURIFIL THREAD   www.aurifil.com

BARI J.   *(Fabrics used on Sweet Tweet Bag)*
barijonline.com

BERNINA SEWING MACHINES
berninausa.com

C&T PUBLISHING   *(Carol Doak's Foundation Paper, fast2fuse HEAVY, Shape-Flex, Wash-Away Appliqué Sheets)*
ctpub.com

DEAR STELLA DESIGN   *(Fabrics used on Out-of-Towner Tote and Hotty Totty Casserole Carrier)*
dearstelladesign.com

DRITZ NOTIONS   dritz.com

GEORGIE EMERSON VINTAGE
georgieemerson.blogspot.com

INTRESSA THREAD
seewhatmaterializes.com

JENNIFER PAGANELLI   *(Fabrics used on Happy Birthday Celebration Shirt, Junior Ranger Backpack, and Bicycle Basket)*
sisboom.com

THE WARM COMPANY
warmcompany.com

QUILTHOME.COM   *(Fabrics and more)*

stash BOOKS®

fabric arts for a handmade lifestyle

If you're craving beautiful authenticity in a time of mass-production...Stash Books is for you. Stash Books is a line of how-to books celebrating fabric arts for a handmade lifestyle. Backed by C&T Publishing's solid reputation for quality, Stash Books will inspire you with contemporary designs, clear and simple instructions, and engaging photography.

www.stashbooks.com